Lifting the Veil of Choice

Defending Life

Lifting the Veil of Choice

Defending Life

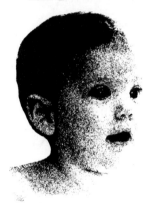

Foreword
by
Mother
Teresa
of
Calcutta

Drew DeCoursey

Our Sunday Visitor Publishing Division
Our Sunday Visitor, Inc.
Huntington, Indiana 46750

Our Sunday Visitor Publishing Division
Our Sunday Visitor, Inc.
200 Noll Plaza
Huntington, Indiana 46750

International Standard Book Number: 0-87973-522-8
Library of Congress Catalog Card Number: 92-90499

Cover design by Monica Watts

PRINTED IN THE UNITED STATES OF AMERICA

522

For

Harry Hand and Peggy Lynch DeCoursey

(". . . in prison, and you visited me")

and

The Missionaries of Charity

. . . who in Jesus' name and for His sake bring love, peace, and joy to the poorest of the poor, born and unborn, throughout the world.

FOREWORD

Jesus became a child to teach us to love the child. And today He comes once again among us as the unborn child, and His own receive Him not. And it is to one of the unborn that God gave the greatness of proclaiming the coming of Christ on earth — the little unborn John in his mother's womb.

The preborn child is the beautiful creation of God, created in His image and likeness for greater things — to love and to be loved. There is no more choice, once a child has been conceived — a second life is in the womb of the mother. To destroy that life by abortion is a murder — worse than any other murder. Because today the preborn are dying by the deliberate will of the ones who have given them life. The preborn child, being so small — so weak — so dependent — so unable to defend its life, is the poorest of the poor.

Abortion is the greatest destroyer of peace in the world today. Therefore, let us do all we can to help every mother want her unborn child, welcome her child as the gift of God's love for her and her family. My prayer is with each of you who read this book, that you allow Jesus to use you more and more as instruments of His peace — the true peace that comes from loving and caring and respecting everyone — even the unborn child.

God bless you
M Teresa MC

Mother Teresa, Missionaries of Charity

7

PREFACE

In working with the urban poor over the past decade, I've learned that poverty extends beyond the need for bread, housing, or jobs. It's true that treasures may sometimes be found in the midst of deprivation. Yet the obverse evidences that poverty of other kinds thrive even in the most privileged neighborhoods of our shared society.

Societal impoverishment extends well beyond the gray reaches of the inner city, climbing up even into the purple-mountained majesties by which the poet symbolizes promise and all that is considered good about our nation. And blight can wither waves of grain, however amber. Color is no protection against any human tragedy.

Since the 1970s, abortion on demand has given rise to an ethical blight on America's nobly declared and fundamental tenet that we each have an inalienable right to life. Instead, the nation's highest court gave us a new and conflicting counter-right which has ever since left this society in a mood of moral stalemate.

About twenty years ago we lowered our eyes from an uplifted view of spacious skies to alleys where we saw evil; and stumbling, we attempted to correct it. But our vision was blurred, and we tried to right a wrong by moving the wrongdoing practitioner's shingle from the darkness of a back alley to the broad daylight of the front porch. Our national purpose in this event seemed not to eliminate the evil, but to elevate it; to scrub it up, dress it in clean garments, call it safe, and introduce a new

9

billion-dollar industry on the backs of troubled young women and their newly deceased children.

Lifting the Veil of 'Choice' is based on writings and certain philosophical musings about the poverty of abortion in contemporary America. This compilation is a mixed marriage of appeals to Christians, to peoples of other faiths, and to secularists. Some of these items have appeared in local organs; some popped up in a few talks. Some have never seen daylight.

A few years ago, a friend suggested I bundle up some of my writings and publish them between two covers like a sandwich. Though interested, I didn't find the time until, recovering from cancer surgery, I discovered a lot of time. So here is the bundle. The fifty or so essays in this book are the outflow of this effort. These writings are purposefully brief and aimed at the busy among us who may not have time to pour through lengthy tomes. Each item should take no more than two or three minutes to read.

Most of these short essays were not crafted as dogmatic sectarian reproach to the tragedy of accepted abortion in society. Rather, they are about logic, good sense, and the need for a return to a consistent life ethos in contemporary pluralistic America. Yet the values projected are undeniably Christian.

At the marrow of these writings is the belief that those who in their hearts support life and oppose abortion must stand up and speak out now. The appeal is to the reader to become more informed and active. Perhaps that action will be as a messenger: not as a bylined journalist necessarily, but as a writer of measured, sensitive letters to elected officials and to your own neighbors through the opinion pages of the local newspaper. People can be influenced and persuaded by the reasonable arguments of others. But if we fail to present an appeal for human life in that portion of our newspaper, there will be no one to counter the overwhelming "pro-choice" bias of the media. If we back away from articulating the need for basic life protections to our representatives in congress, the state legislatures, and even our local governments, we will have lost the day. For surely our politicians will accede to the demands of the powerful apologists for abortion — and now euthanasia. Then, when laws edge even beyond today's step-by-step, selected executions of the least of our innocent brothers and sisters, to whom will we cling for our own escape?

We are each gifted in some manner. We are all of great value. There is no one who is not. To say otherwise would give credence to those who promote abortion, euthanasia, and other methods to eliminate what they consider to be "life devoid of value."

The task is left to each of us. We need to act: peacefully, lovingly, nonviolently, and now.

Like others, I am indebted to John Cavanaugh-O'Keefe of Maryland for his peaceful, nonviolent, but boldly courageous leadership and example of unselfish love for God and humanity at a time when the national pro-life movement most needed a transfusion of Type A positive direct action. He helped nurture me from silent resignation to outspoken activism. A gifted writer blessed with a keen mind and gentle heart (a combination in the best tradition of Irish poets), JCOK embodies for me the spirit of Pope Paul VI's words: If you want peace, work for justice.

THE RIGHT TO FREE CHOICE is tightly woven into the fabric of American life. The very nature of a republic proclaims the right to choose our leaders and representatives. Who among us could oppose "choice," a word that rings of freedom and opportunity in an open society? And yet, to our misfortune, we are often taken in by the veil of "choice."

Isn't it profoundly essential to know the meaning of our choices before we choose? The "right to choose" sounds noble. But if we don't dig deeper to unearth what the choices truly are, and what consequences they bring, we are simply responding to pleasant sounds and might better spend our time listening to Brahms.

In the case of abortion or the increasing incidence of state- and hospital-sanctioned infanticide, "choice" can be grim. To abort or not to abort, to the victim, means to die or to live. Quite a significant choice! Do we favor the continuance of four thousand death choices daily throughout the United States?

Perhaps we are anesthetized by many words and euphemisms. We seem to favor the word "choice" over "death to an innocent preborn human being"; "product of conception" over "child"; "termination of pregnancy" over "killing a fetus"; and "unwanted child" over "a joy to adoptive parents."

Someone has said that all genetic engineering is preceded by verbal engineering. "Pro-choice" means either "pro-death" or "take your pick; either selection — life or death — is okay with me."

Some of us once believed in the brother/sisterhood of

humankind. If this is still true and each living human being is still our sister or our brother, how can we "choose" to allow or actively support their deaths?

To say we are "pro-choice" on abortion (an act resulting in a death) is to say we don't care whether people choose to put others to death or allow them to live. It's their choice; either is acceptable, we say. So, in a sense, both are equally to be tolerated.

Yet there is no choice equal to life. Death is not the equal to life, but rather its ultimate antithesis. If there is truly choice in this people-caring society, we ought to consider carefully and choose life.

In HER NOBEL PEACE PRIZE acceptance speech, Mother Teresa upset some people by singling out abortion as the greatest destroyer of peace in the world today. Some critics felt she should have limited her remarks to reflections on poverty. Yet that is precisely what this woman, who knows poverty intimately, was saying. Abortion sanctioned by the state reflects a policy of spiritual impoverishment.

There are many Americans who believe we are impoverished when we encourage and permit, under protection of law, the capricious pruning of our own next generation. The oldest of those who luckily escaped the pruning process established by Roe v. Wade are now nineteen years old — my son's age.

One wonders if these children will one day turn and ask us about their sisters and brothers who are no more. Parents may be asked by their children why they were spared and if the circumstances of convenience differed, might they too have been sacrificed to some modern Molech? How will we answer?

Again, one wonders about the increase in child abuse, child pornography, disturbing revelations from child-care centers and the disappearance of so many young children in the past decade.

But should we be surprised? If we can abuse to death our developing children at nine weeks or nine months, why not at nine years?

Not all poverty is simply the lack of bread or shelter. The cruelest poverty and one over which we have control is the one we deliberately inflict on our young. It is the spiritual poverty of our generation which violates the right to continue, uninterrupted by outside force, that life which has already begun.

Social scientists tell us that our society has reached an imbalance between generations. The older are becoming more numerous; the younger more scarce. Even retirement is in jeopardy. It is the young workers who pay the Social Security benefits of the retired. It soon may happen that the young may no longer be able, or willing, to pay for the old. As our generation moves beyond productivity into retirement, we may find it is we who have become inconvenient. And the young may impose on the mature what we taught them through the fruits of Roe v. Wade: if a life is inconvenient, we may choose to terminate it.

Those of us who eluded the abortionist's scalpel may find we are hoist at last by our own petard through involuntary euthanasia imposed by those to whom we justified abortion.

THE SUPREME COURT ruled that a human fetus is not a "person" and may be terminated at its mother's choice. The state of Minnesota ruled that an 8½-month-old fetus is not a "human being" and her life may be terminated with impunity by a drunk driver. And she was.

This precedent seems to extend to everyone, at least in Minnesota, a right to terminate the life of anyone else's fetus regardless of the mother's choice.

Meanwhile, the developing bird life within an eagle's egg is protected by federal and state laws, and a stiff fine or imprisonment may accompany its destruction.

So much for choice. So much for the sanctity of human life.

INTO **THE ALLEY OF DEATH** strode the tens of thousands. At their flank as they advanced stood a grim, red-faced line: firing targeted volleys of noxious invective at the marchers-by.

On the Abortionists' Feast Day, January 22, nearly a hundred thousand men, women, and children walked in solidarity for the nineteenth time down Washington's Constitution Avenue in celebration of all human life, and in outrage for nearly two decades of abortion on demand that had snuffed out so many innocent lives in this nation dedicated at its outset to an inalienable right to life. But this year the march was different.

For a stretch along Constitution Avenue, organized hundreds of abortion supporters broke the chill winter air with the heat of hate-shouted anger. The Marchers for Life were mocked and cursed; nothing new there.

But the pro-abortion counter-demonstrators had been tightly organized for 1992. They screamed and blew shrill whistles. They held up signs reading: "Get Your Religion Out Of My Crotch!" and, contradictorily, involved their crotches and placards in religion with a curiously scribbled epithet: "Mary — Safe Sex Slut!"

Among the pro-life marchers was a young woman named Mary Oswald who, with a number of companions, found herself a curbstone away from the angry mob. Mary was participating in her sixth March for Life. And in her case, active participation involves deep faith, love of life, and personal courage — both physical and moral — that is an inspiration to anyone who meets her. Mary completed the march in a wheelchair pushed by a friend.

A congenital amputee, Mary was born without fully developed limbs. She is quick to point out that she is not a "thalidomide baby" as some people may have assumed.

"God, who can do all things," Mary reminds us, "knew I would be born this way, yet permitted it." She accepts that her disability is "part of God's plan."

A strong, practicing Catholic Christian, Mary says, "Jesus taught us that we must pick up our own cross and follow him. This is my cross; I try to do my best to follow Christ's example. I believe that good will come from this."

The eldest of six children of a remarkable mother and father, Mary Oswald is a pretty and bright young woman trained as a professional counselor. She has a bachelor's degree in psychology and a master's degree in vocational-rehabilitation counseling. Mary drives her own car to work at The Matheny School and Hospital in Peapack, New Jersey. In her free time, Mary contributes her beautiful singing voice to her parish, where she participates both as song leader and as a member of the church choir. This gifted and cheerful young woman has performed as featured soloist at pro-life conventions and rallies in New Jersey and Pennsylvania. Few hearing Mary sing "How Great Thou Art" can remain unaffected.

But this day in January 1992 she was marching in the cold of the nation's capital. Mary looked into the faces of the pro-abortion demonstrators and saw hate and livid anger. Although somewhat frightened, Mary hoped her presence would change at least one heart in the screaming mob. She wanted to show them somehow that life is important; that it is worth living no matter what. So, in that cold air, she loosened her coat and pulled up her sleeve so that counter-demonstrators could see her arm, which ends at the elbow. Mary looked into their faces and slowly shook her head in disapproval. And she simply said, "Life!"

Several of those whose eyes met hers stopped screaming, at least for the moment. "It took a lot of strength for me to confront them, lovingly; but I did it," says Mary.

"I believe," says Mary, "that so many of them are caught up in their own bodies. They seem to be ignorant that life is a gift from God, and that we each should do the best we can with what we have."

This courageous young woman, whom a friend describes as "loveliness, both inside and out," for a moment broke through the dissonant air to interject a sign of peace and hope for those whose anger is often too loud to be pierced by gentle conviction. Mary was holy water to their eyes. These are not all bad people, Mary would agree; but like many, they seem snagged on the shoals of a bad tide. However, tides go out as tides come in, and in the affairs of mankind as well as the sea, a new tide can be a cleansing thing.

Marches move along in a determined direction. And as the marchers (no less determined) continued along our national Via Dolorosa, Mary hoped that one heart in that angry crowd may have calmed and softened because she or he saw the deep claim that Mary makes to her life. The empty argument of unwanted children and disabled lives is washed bare by the new tide.

Other March-for-Life participants stepped past the shouting, whistle-blowing hecklers of that grim red-faced line: loud, angry, hateful, collective, but dispirited. The anti-life scream is discordant, acting out the despair of those whose ill-starred cause once peaked but now (they fear) wanes; a shrill, mocking, shrieking crowd of lonely hundreds bound only each to self, without spiritual anchor or purpose beyond the last frantic clutchings at an expiring license.

As the life marchers moved ahead up the hill toward their destination, some were keenly aware that the intensity of screaming behind them seemed lessened and then faded from sound. And when the marchers turned, the abortion supporters could be seen vaguely, silently motionless in the distance, like a dark, dead moon forever locked in orbit outside a thriving, moving planet.

"We need to reach out," says Mary Oswald. We need to pray and sacrifice for their conversions, while continuing ourselves to be witnesses for the preborn." These are the selfless thoughts of a young woman who works with many who might be considered unwanted, devoid of value, or disabled.

So who is it that is disabled? Not Mary. At least not in the larger sense. She's as whole as any being. It's the spirit that drives the body. Philosophers have long known this. The history and culture of our human race records only the deeds of the abled. Helen Keller was able, as was the crippled Franklin Roosevelt. Beethoven, Stevie Wonder, Stephen Hawking, Christy Brown are listed among those who have added bright chapters to our history and culture. Yet would our society, which seems to want only the perfect, make an investment in advance on today's unborns who share the same imperfections as these noted contributors? Isn't that part of the controversy?

Early in 1992, *The New York Times* ran a front-page feature glorifying the late-term abortion efforts of Warren Hern and George Tiller, who specialize in ending babies' lives in as late as their prenatal eighth and ninth months for reasons which include Down Syndrome and other imperfections. Such words as "compassionate" and "heroic" found their way into the feature. The *Times* quotes Hern: "This is a very difficult area of medicine. You have to make a decision that's part ethical, part moral."

Which part is which? Of course, the article doesn't say. Nor does it say that the disabilities overcome by those cultural contributors listed by me two paragraphs back might make them prime targets for extinction today. Yet as Dr. Hern might add, the decisions to end innocent lives would be "part ethical, part moral." Or was that Dr. Josef Mengele?

To my mind, Mary Oswald will reach spiritual perfection before Hern, Tiller, or others who misguidedly destroy human life. The view in front of Mary's perfect vision is of life, not death. She spends her working day counseling and guiding young people who have imperfections and disabilities of wide variance and variety. She's often tough on her students, placing realistically high expectations on them because that's how she was raised.

If pressed, Mary prioritizes her thankfulness to the God who made each of us, perhaps not perfect, yet in His own image and likeness. Mary is thankful for her life, her faith, and her family. Next, she is thankful for her abilities and her disabilities: "I use both to the fullest, as best I can."

For this young woman apostle for life, perfection lies ahead. "For now," she says, "this is how God wants me to be. He says, 'You are good this way and for our purpose, hidden though it may be now. We are holding your limbs for you in Heaven. But it's up to you to get here to claim them.' "

Mary Oswald knows choice; she has chosen great faith, or rather has been gifted with it. We are promised that true faith will make us whole. Mary's long-awaited gifts will not go unclaimed.

"Martha, Martha," Jesus said, "you worry and fret about so many things, and yet few are needed, indeed only one. It is Mary who has chosen the better part; it is not to be taken from her."

Among the Surgeon General's **DISTRESS SIGNALS** tagged onto cigarette advertising is this one: "Smoking by Pregnant Women May Result in Fetal Injury." This strange mix of appeals, to have your child and smoke it too, seems perversely characteristic of our age.

More recently, the government's medical cops added a similar warning label to alcoholic beverages. It is gratifying that our top medical officers acknowledge the need to protect the preborn child from possible injury.

Advertisers commit big bucks in attracting us to destroy ourselves, then remind us that we're also destroying our soon-to-be children — whom the abortion laws say we may destroy anyhow. Yet in its promotion of dangerous substances, the tobacco and alcohol industries inadvertently send up a pro-life flare.

The Surgeon General's unfiltered message is that Mom may be crippling her fetal-stage child. In the post-birth stages of the same child's development, Mom's abuse may send her to jail; but for now, she can generally do as she wishes with her child's life. Shouldn't that strike us as odd?

Logic dictates that if my preborn fetus is injured and untreated, then my post-born child will likewise possess the same injury. That should give a rather strong clue that the preborn fetus and the post-born child are the one-and-the-same, unique individual human life which Roe v. Wade balks at calling a "person."

Yet if this is so obvious, why do we Americans continue to destroy our children in the fetal stage at the

24

rate of one every twenty-two seconds every day? Despite loud noises from pro-abortion-choice supporters, science does not equivocate but tells us that the preborn child is alive, human, and male or female, having twenty-three chromosomes from the mother and a like number from the dad. That's why the tobacco and whiskey industries have to adjust their marketing strategies regarding pregnant women. It's not pro-life organizations imposing this prenatal care; it's medical science backed by the U.S. government.

Tobacco and alcohol advertisers are forced to be somewhat candid in referencing the dangers of the products they promote. This is good. But now it's time for a Surgeon General's warning to accompany abortion-services ads. After all, abortion, like smoking and drinking by pregnant women, may result in "fetal injury." In fact, with abortion it's guaranteed!

A suggested callout for abortion ads and clinic signs: "Abortions on Pregnant Women Will Result in Fetal Injury." Namely, death.

OLD WAYS DON'T CHANGE until new demands force confrontations. Consider this: In various cities, groups of citizens espousing a sometimes-unpopular cause block building entrances and pester certain profitable enterprises operating as legally protected business. Owners of affected businesses point to this legal status and accuse protesters of trespass. Police are summoned and protestors are hauled off to jail. For their part, the protestors claim that the law is wrong and quote time-honored declarations that all are created equal, with inalienable rights that civil law may not breach.

The issue divides the nation into two camps. Some look to the Supreme Court in hope, others in fear. And even some who support the moral views of the protesters are unhappy with acts of civil disobedience. To many, such actions appear to be deliberate lawbreaking intended to impose protesters' views on other people.

But what if the protesters are right and the law in question is indeed wrong? Laws don't change by themselves. Unless some action is taken somewhere by someone, what is called "legal," although morally repugnant, continues as law.

These acts of protest occurred in the South of the 1960s. Similar events occurred in Wichita in the summer of 1991. But they appeared first in other seasons in other cities such as Montgomery, Birmingham, Selma. In those earlier seasons, the law protected restaurants, bus companies, and other businesses whose practices, though legal at the time, violated the humanity and dignity of a class of people. When enough ordinary citizens found extraordinary courage to protest injustice and endure beatings, jail, lawsuits, charges of conspiracy, and ridicule by their neighbors, then things did change.

Things continue to change. Bad law cannot long stand the test of time. Laws resulting in the ongoing deaths of a class of innocent individuals will fall; injustice ultimately buckles under the weight of unmasked truth. And unlike that monkey who stands in doubtful guard at the gate of Nikko, society will remove its hands from over its eyes and see the evident evil. Then society in this good republic will fix it.

THE **COMMENTATOR** who concluded that a human fetus is of little consequence because preborns are not included in U. S. Census should not be taken too seriously. He is just having fun. But he is correct in saying that the child waiting to be born is not included in the census. But so what? Neither are foreign tourists. Yet they live and can reasonably expect that their safety will be safeguarded while vacationing in this country. Prior to this latest census, all American kids nine years old and younger weren't counted either since the census only comes around every ten years. Were they not human these early years of their childhood?

Our humanity rests not with the Census Bureau, nor the Supreme Court. In the founding document of our republic, Jefferson paraphrased Rousseau about certain inalienable rights residual to our human nature, endowed by nature's Author. Jefferson and his colleagues concurred in this Declaration thirteen years before the U. S. Constitution became law, and fourteen years before creation of the first census of U. S. population. It may be assumed that in those years people were considered as existing without being officially tabulated by a government agency.

The commentator of choice is an intelligent person and well aware that the product of two humans can only be another human, not an eagle's egg or a baby seal (wait a minute! I believe they are protected by law). The commentator knows also that the human fetus is a developing child who received at conception a genetic package consisting of twenty-three chromosomes from the mother and (often forgotten) twenty-three chromosomes from the father. So, the humanity of the fetus is not really in question; in essence, it's the answer.

This exponent of choice intends simply to point up that the government no longer provides protections to the preborn human in nine months of the first year of development. However, we are aware of emphasis being made by both government and health professionals to improve prenatal care. Prenatal means "preborn" and neither is covered by the census, this time. Pro-life people work so that prenatals will be around to be counted in the next census.

Pregnant women are counseled, by authorities ranging from the Surgeon General to virtually everyone else, to avoid drugs, tobacco, and alcohol so the child will have a better chance of remaining healthy at birth.

Our commentator is being cute about the role of the Supreme Court. This judicial body did not, as he says, conclude that the fetus is not a human being. The Court said (sadly) that the preborn is "not a person in the sense of the Constitution." Until that 1973 decision, the fetus was accorded certain protections of law. For example, abortionists were put in jail. Today, those who would save the fetus from death are put in jail.

One of the more glaring insensitivities the census commentator makes could dredge up painful historical memories for African-Americans. He stands unwittingly at the threshold of racism. He doesn't intend hurt, but consider: until the latter part of the last century, people not free (e.g., slaves) were not rated in the census as whole persons in the sense of the Constitution. Article I, Section 2 of the Constitution says the census provides the data for congressional representation and taxes, and those not free are counted as "three-fifths" of a person. That didn't change until the Thirteenth Amendment (1865), and the Fourteenth (1868) provided constitutional redress and franchise to African-Americans. It's true, too, that "Indians not taxed" were not even counted in the early U. S. Census.

Allow the commentator to enjoy his exercise in goat-getting; it is of little moment to the true issue. While he writes a good letter, his view of U.S. history and human life need enlightenment.

A LETTER FROM FORTY MEMBERS OF CLERGY praising County Freeholders for giving public funds to Planned Parenthood gives reason for pause.

Across the country, the national Planned Parenthood organization includes abortion as a major reproductive care offering. In the case of some Planned Parenthood affiliates, the organization makes referrals to physicians who, according to accepted application of the law, may abort the preborn at any age — from detection to nine months. In other locales, Planned Parenthood actively sponsors abortuaries where innocent human life is tragically ended.

It has been cited elsewhere that Planned Parenthood is the largest single provider of abortion in America. Yet the clergy group's letter unfortunately makes no disclaimer concerning these abortion-related services. Perhaps this was an oversight.

Otherwise, it might appear that the strongly supportive clergy letter endorses the full package of options open to interpretation under "reproductive health care . . . services," including abortion. Such an acceptance might be construed as analogous to arguing for reinvestment in the South African government because they build fine roads.

I should like to believe that somewhere among the forty signers of the clergy letter, there are some who reject abortion as conflicting with moral precepts found in Deuteronomy, Isaiah, Jeremiah, Luke, and elsewhere in Scripture.

TWO **QUESTIONS** for Christian clergy wavering on a critical issue: if Planned Parenthood had counseled in Galilee about 2,000 years ago, what might the advice have been to the pregnant, unwed, teenaged Mary?

And of course Mary would not have listened or consented, but if she could have, what would you be doing for a living today?

ON THE SAME DAY the Supreme Court struck down a Pennsylvania state law that provided information to women considering abortion, the New Jersey State Board of Medical Examiners barred an East Hanover physician from performing abortions following charges that his procedures resulted in the death of one teenager and injuries to another.

The same abortionist had previously been restricted in his work because of three other alleged injuries to young women.

There are some interesting overlaps in the actions of both the court and the board. The intent of the Pennsylvania law was not to "intimidate" women with the facts but, as recognized in the Roe v. Wade decision, to allow states after the first trimester to regulate abortion procedures in ways reasonably related to maternal health.

Now it would seem that informing a young woman of medical risks involved in abortion is "reasonably related" to her pregnancy and her health; and her right to sufficient information is essential to arrive at fully informed consent.

The East Hanover episode appears to bear this out. The New Jersey attorney general's office charged that the doctor violated state laws by performing in-office abortions past the first trimester. State regulations require that these abortions be performed in a hospital.

Did the young women who are the alleged victims know this? It would be interesting to know how well informed these women were when they gave their "informed consent" to these abortions.

Yet, the Court decision rendered by Judge Blackmun now overrides what he himself pronounced in Roe! Now, he tells America, factual information provided to a young woman to help her reach an informed consent is not permissible because knowing there are medical risks in abortion can "increase the patient's anxiety" concerning that which she is about to do.

So rather than risk that upset, it is more relevant to her rights to be kept in the dark. On one hand, she may be upset; on the other she may be maimed.

The East Hanover case is even more bizarre when one considers the time frame. The doctor is charged with performing the abortion that allegedly caused the death of a fourteen-year-old girl in 1983. And a sixteen-year-old girl was alleged to have sustained uterine injury from abortion the next year.

And yet, until June 1986, he was permitted by the State Board of Medical Examiners and legal authorities to continue to practice his abortion rites. In April, this doctor had been limited to first-trimester abortions because of alleged injuries to three other abortion patients in 1985 and early 1986.

How long does it take and how many injuries must be sustained by women before action is taken?

Informed consent? How many women would have consented to abortion by this practitioner if they had been informed of his alleged history?

WHO **ARE OUR HEROES?** The rock star, the actor, the athlete? The brash, the sexy, the wealthy? These are often venerated by our young people as paradigms of success and worthy of emulation. Among adult citizens, hero selection is more circumspect.

Let me tell you about a young woman named Gay who may not be so widely known within the national pro-life movement. But she was there early to speak out and to act; she took her stand, and her lumps, and without ever knowing it became a gentle hero to those who observed and marveled at her almost silent, self-effacing grace.

But background first: Years before the days of Operation Rescue, a small group of rescuers (we called them sit-ins then) succeeded in a series of nonviolent challenges to the powerful abortion industry in Maryland. The objective was simple: save a woman and her child from the arsenal of the abortionist in the only way open to the unempowered. The method was the nonviolent sit-in borrowed from the peace movement, which in turn borrowed it from the civil rights movement, which learned it from Gandhi, that apostle of nonviolence and human rights. The weapon was the temporary sacrifice of one's own body and liberty.

Gay began challenging the horror of "choice" when one of her own sisters nearly died from a botched abortion. Gay often stood by the entrance to the abortuary, tears streaming down her cheeks, as she tried to dissuade other young women from the pain of her own sister's fate. Gay is like a sun shower; the water issues easily over the light of her gentle face. She would counsel softly, lovingly, and if that failed, would block the door with her body. She was arrested, jailed, fined, yet always gave heroic witness at her own trials. Often she rescued by herself or with two or three others. But the example of this woman and her likewise courageous companions inspired others to join in the effort to save lives.

In time, Gay married and had her own babies, yet continued her rescue work. At one large sit-in during that Orwellian summer of 1984, Gay's sister and others not participating in the action watched from the safety of a public sidewalk as the demonstration unfolded. Her sister held firm to Gay's baby.

With others, Gay was arrested and led by police to a patrol van where other rescuers were already shackled and crammed inside. Police insisted she place her hands behind her back to be handcuffed for the ride to jail; Gay obeyed. She hesitated at the door of the van, scanning the bystanders for her family. Her sister approached holding Gay's young son in her arms and received a policeman's permission to talk with Gay. Then ensued a brief woman-to-woman exchange on feeding the child at such-and-such time, the whereabouts of clean diapers in the bag, and so forth, as two police officers manacled the hands of this young mother. Although the baby reached out for her, Gay could not respond since her hands were locked behind her back. "Kiss him for me," the whispered good-bye seemed to say. And again, the silent tears at separation.

To at least one person already manacled in the van, a clear symbolism emerged from the scene. Here was a compassionate mother in love with her child and pained by a forced separation. Yet neither complaint nor regret issued even once from her. The tears flowed, but no sobs

36

and no blame, only a mother's smile. And despite her own discomfort and inconvenience, this mom assured the child's safety, care, and placement with the right person before the loading of prisoners could continue.

Gay survived, and the baby survived as we all survive, or most of us. But the anonymous, frightened, and troubled young woman who carries the ripening fruit of her womb into the abortion chamber emerges alone and too often scarred. If only she could run into a sun shower and speak first with Gay before effecting that terrible choice.

NOT LONG AGO, New Jersey state officials sought an acceptable method for dispensing death by capital punishment. New Jersey and other states prepared again for the business of killing people.

Like others, I am troubled by any life-taking, even if those to be executed may be guilty of a crime against society. But the greatest horror, to my mind, is participation by the state and federal governments in the taking of innocent human life; and this has been going on at an alarming rate since 1973. I refer, of course, to legalized capital punishment of innocents through abortion. These victims have committed no crime, have broken no law. Their only offense seems to be that they are inconvenient.

A former governor suggested lethal injections, perhaps by physicians, as the preferred method of administering capital punishment to criminals in my state. Physicians and the medical profession reacted with indignation, citing their role as healers and not executioners. I agree, and I applaud and support their position. However, the medical profession is neither reluctant nor outraged by its willing participation in administering lethal injections (e.g., saline solution) into innocent preborn human life.

Physicians routinely perform abortions, contrary to the Hippocratic Oath, once held in esteem by the healing profession. It is argued that doctors, lawyers, and theologians cannot agree specifically on when life begins (but this is changing; consider recent success in fetal surgery). Yet in practice, and to the exclusion of millions of lives, we have demonstrated that we simply don't care.

We say: if a pregnancy occurs and is inconvenient, terminate (kill) it.

In his minority opinion in Roe v. Wade, Justice Byron White clearly warned us that, since well-intentioned and learned men and women cannot agree on the beginnings of human life, we ought not to select any time theory as justification lest we choose the wrong one. He expressed his position that the Supreme Court, of which he is a member, is not qualified to make a determination on such a life-and-death moral question. Suppose, as Justice White seemed to fear, we one day learn we have chosen the wrong course. What then should be our recompense? And what has been our gain? Will we as a generation and our decision makers be judged at some future Nuremberg?

Now we have reintroduced capital punishment. Now even the guilty may suffer the life loss we have routinely meted out to the young, crimeless innocents since 1973.

It's an interesting scenario: is there a chance that this nation, which for years has protected from death many adjudged guilty, will now make a similarly ironic reversal and protect those innocent lives which for so many years it has agreed may be put to death?

A **HEADLINE, CRYING** "Two Babies Discovered in Trash," reports on two newborn girls found in New York trash bins just hours after their births. One girl survived and is being cared for; the other was barely alive when discovered but died soon after. A spokesman for the Transit Police said that while the cause of death of the young victim was not determined, there were "no indications of foul play."

Think about that: a newborn baby found in a trash can, but no suspicion of foul play. Does the spokesman attempt to leave room that the baby's death and disposal may have been self-inflicted — a rare newborn suicide? Or are we so inured to the abuse of our children that we fail to fathom that somewhere between her mother's pregnancy and the garbage pail, something foul happened to that child.

And something, too, has happened within the last two decades to our own innate sense of care and protection for new life. Consider the stories of abuse, neglect, abandonment, abortion, and infanticide that fill our news pages. Why such little regard for human life?

The positive wrinkle to this story is that one of the baby girls survived and is in stable condition, hopefully on the way to take her rightful place in this world. At least she now has that chance, owing to the kindness of a homeless stranger who, rummaging through a trash barrel, found a new life and perhaps redeemed another.

SOME WILL ARGUE that a woman has a right to do what she will with her own body. Laws against suicide and drug use make that assertion somewhat moot. My major concern would be that no other innocent body be hurt when an adult exercises options to his or her own body. Science doesn't equivocate on the question of difference between a mother's body and that of the offspring being nourished and sheltered within her. The two are separate. Their blood systems are separate, as are their hearts and other organs and their genetic makeup.

In the clamor over my good mother's rights to her own body, I would hope that she doesn't do anything unpleasant to mine as it rests in the only shelter that nature provides for me or any mother's child in those critical preborn days.

IN A RECENT LETTER, a well-respected minister shared his distress that Judge Noonan's now-famous Morristown trial findings somehow "imposed his narrow religious beliefs on everyone else."

My reading of the case is somewhat different. Neither the judge's deliberations nor his decision contains any reference to religion, narrow or otherwise. What the judge did allow was testimony of highly recognized medical-science experts including a world-renowned geneticist and an ob/gyn from Cornell — both of whom presented scientific evidence that life begins at conception.

Yet it is the offended minister who raises the specter of religion. Religious tolerance is not well-served when a minister asserts that the bogeyman of another religion (we all know which one is implied) is behind a judge's decision. How does he know this when the impacting testimony is scientific only? It's also fact that no scientist came forward to say under oath that life, which confers "personhood," does *not* begin at conception.

The minister says "human life begins when the fetus can live on its own." But a newborn in the intensive care nursery may find she is unable to live on her own without breath from a temporary respirator. Is she not "alive" during this dependent period?

Wise man, riddle me this: If a fetus is not alive, then why do we kill it? And what will result if we don't kill it? We need only to look into a mirror, or at our own child. In each case we see life at a different stage: one mature and independent, perhaps even fading; the other unempowered, dependent and developing toward the next stage. Yet both claim human life and share a historical journey through the embryonic, fetal, newborn, baby, infant, adolescent, and whatever life stages follow naturally until a life-taking event occurs.

Why do we hold such genuine concern for prenatal care if the fetus is not alive, not human? Surely, proper prenatal care is necessary; even cigarette ads affirm that. Yet how can a human fetus be alive when we're tempted by tobacco but not alive when abortion is the interest? Again the convenient and flexible "person" argument. Isn't it odd that all members of the family of corporations enjoy protected "person" status, but not all members of the human family?

Consider the man on the iron lung, the woman with an artificial heart, a child on a respirator: each is dependent for life on some support outside of self. Are these people no longer "persons," no longer alive? This country got into a heap of trouble during the last century because of its application of the word "person." We'd be better advised and far more honest to focus on the reality of "human life" while leaving obfuscation of "person" to corporate lawyers and distress to the clergy. Science has ruled when human life begins; the judge simply reported it.

SURELY IT ISN'T REQUIRED that one personally take in the homeless before speaking out on homelessness.

To abhor violence, one need not assume a Zen lifestyle.

To fight AIDS, one is not compelled to embrace homosexuality or a needle.

Then why do we challenge pro-lifers to adopt all the kids in the world in exchange for speaking out to spare their lives?

The exercise of free speech prompted by recognition of naked injustice bears no cost of admission. Not in this republic.

THE NEW YORK CITY BOARD OF EDUCATION, once renowned for dispensing education, has bartered away much of its declining stock in exchange for latex futures. The chancellor and board of the nation's largest school system can now dole out condoms on demand to children at one hundred twenty schools as part of an effort to reduce the incidence of AIDS, and secondarily teenage pregnancy and abortion. Noble end; bizarre means.

A request by some New York City parents to deny condom access to their own children was itself denied by the board and Chancellor Fernandez.

In logic approaching that of the emperor in the buff, Dr. Fernandez waved off any consideration of the "Just Say No" message of abstinence to avoid sexually acquired AIDS. Instead, New York City schools now offer a tax-funded tool tacitly encouraging teen sexual activity which could lead to an increase of the very disease they hope to reduce. "Just say yes, but wear this first."

Planned Parenthood's sex watchers calculate a failure rate of as much as eighteen percent for condom use. That's one in six condom users playing unsafe sex. Russian roulette is played by hiding a round in one of a revolver's six chambers, then pointing it at one's own head and squeezing the trigger. Same odds.

Curious scenarios may ensue: "Johnny" accepts the school's latex handouts and health protection claims, then contracts a sexually transmitted horror such as AIDS, syphilis, or other venereal disease from Susie or Phil.

Since parental notification is precluded from the school's condom caper, Ma and Pa are unaware of Johnny's after-school activity (they thought he had a paper route). Now they know; Johnny was the one in six. Enter the legal profession; Ma and Pa bring an expensive suit against the city, its school board, the chancellor, the school nurse, condom suppliers, plus Susie and/or Phil's parents. Whether the city or the family wins, a new tragedy enters the curriculum: Johnny definitely loses.

Once upon a time, schools dispensed the "Three R's." Today, another "R" meets the road passing through the muddied field of American education. Perhaps New York City next envisions dispensing free hypodermic needles to schoolkids to ward off drug-related AIDS; so much for "just say no." It's an unfortunate admission of lack of hope in our youth when schools give up on dispensing academic knowledge and lessons of self control which could help guide kids through the minefields of life.

Wasn't it less worrisome when kids used to bolt behind the barn for a cigarette?

WE HAVE BECOME ANTENNAE for mixed messages and seem remarkably comfortable in our incongruity. We pursue loud causes against unjust oppressions in some parts of the world (although not all) and protest maltreatment of humans halfway around the globe while watching the growing ubiquity of our own homeless and poor.

We fight for the right to life of whales, timber wolves, the praying mantis, and preborn birds. We resist capital punishment for our murderers, yet show disregard for innocent human life when it causes inconvenience. As a nation and individually, we permit the ongoing carnage of guiltless human lives each day. How can sentiments of our compassion for the children of Africa, Asia, and Latin America be believed when we knowingly trash our own offspring at a rate of 1.5 million each year?

Do we really care about apartheid and Tiananmen Square and El Salvador? Or are these simply safe causes that are fashionable, convenient, and far away.

As AMERICAN SLAVERY STRUGGLED to
survive in the nineteenth century, it was boosted by the
Supreme Court's 1857 ruling that black slaves were not
persons with rights under the Constitution.

Insistence on choice in abortion recalls yesteryear's
debate and eventual war over choice vis-à-vis human
slavery. Consider these analogous events: The Court's
Dred Scott decision officially wrote off
African-Americans as property of those whites who opted
for slavery. At the nub of states and property rights was
the question of "choice." Proponents of the institution of
slavery could boast legal acceptance and even point to a
major court decision for ensuring constitutionally
approved status.

Among those favoring choice on slave owning,
Stephen Douglas, Democratic senator from Illinois, took
the position that slavery was a private matter and
nobody's business outside of the South. Others who
supported choice in this matter, even if personally
opposed to slavery, resented what they perceived as
abolitionists imposing their own morality.

Abolitionists held that since slavery was
fundamentally unjust regardless of the Supreme Court's
finding, there could be no vacillation on choice; one was
either for slavery or against it. Lincoln said as much. To
accept the option of slave owning was recognized as
supporting that tragic though then-constitutional choice.

Having no part in this debate, although it most directly
concerned them, were the third-party victims, the slaves
themselves. The rightness or wrongness of slavery was

48

argued by white people on both sides of the issue, but African-Americans lacked empowerment to speak on their own behalf. Sure, they were human and innocent, but slaves were voiceless and without franchise. The American slave lived or died at the whim of others. And so it is today with the preborn in ironic parallel. Though clearly alive and human, the child in the womb is a powerless third-party victim too often overlooked in the rancorous debate over the choice of abortion.

African-Americans today, recalling their great-grandparents, forthrightly tell us what they think of those nineteenth-century citizens who argued that slave owning was a matter of private choice. But aborted human fetuses won't have grandchildren to recall any familial injustice.

The naked question today is not whether one is pro-choice on abortion, any more than it was one hundred thirty years ago whether one was pro-choice on legal slavery. The real question again rests on Supreme Court-sanctioned property rights over another human's life.

Perhaps the Wichita pro-life demonstrators mirror not 1950s segregationists as a *New York Times* story implies, but rather 1850s abolitionists who acknowledged that acceptance of "choice" in slavery actually accredited and perpetuated that institution.

Through the horror of internecine bloodshed, the slavery question was resolved. Let's hope that human wisdom and changed hearts prevail and we find a better way to respect all human life as precisely the great inalienable gift it is.

To **CHRISTIANS**, John the Baptizer closes the loop of prophecy leading to the promised Messiah. John becomes the ultimate herald by announcing the coming of Christ and ushering in the Christian era which continues today, nearly two millennia later, and will flourish until the end of time. That, at least, is the backdrop of our creed.

John's witness at Jesus' baptism in the Jordan is recalled in each of the four Gospels. But Scripture also tells us that, earlier, John had leapt in the womb of his mother, Elizabeth, when she heard the voice of Mary, who was pregnant with Jesus. So John's first encounter with Jesus was when each was a "nonviable" fetus. This should speak to us that God holds high the value of a child in the womb even if one mother is an unwed teenager and the other is in "her old age," well beyond the ticking of any biological clock.

John the Baptist's prenatal acknowledgment of his Messianic Cousin places him in a unique position to be the patron of preborn babies and developing fetuses. The Baptist's own unjust dismemberment at the hands of Herod and family qualifies as a victory for convenience and choice. But his birth and life were glorious. Jesus called John the Baptist "the greatest man born to woman." Much of the credit must go to Mary and Elizabeth, two women who made the natural choice for their and our own salvation.

JOAN ANDREWS **IS AN UNUSUAL PERSON** in the sense that she is a Christian genuinely committed to saving lives as specifically commanded in Holy Writ when it says of the innocents: "Rescue those who are being led to their executions." That Scriptural injunction is not mitigated for us by any reich, any congress, any court anywhere. We all know this. The difference is that Joan lives it and, if she must, is prepared to suffer for it.

While on trial in Maryland, Joan gently told the judge: "When we do direct action we are confronting the law head on because it is an illegitimate law at its foundation. I've never broken any law . . . even a parking violation. The only times I've been arrested is in trying to save a human life. Deep in my roots I can't believe I will be found guilty in court, but I keep being found guilty. I can't believe people don't understand that children are dying."

The judge replied, "That's what makes my job so difficult." No doubt it is difficult for those who know better but cling to a value they know is false. Joan knows and lives Christ's love and faith even if it means jail. Foolish? Perhaps.

Chesterton observed that one who has faith must be prepared not only to be a martyr, but to be a fool. And what is a saint but a fool for Christ. Is Joan a "fool" in that sense? I hope so.

It was Joan's example that lifted Bishop Austin Vaughan out of the protective comfort of his New York rectory to sit on rough sidewalks in front of aborturies. And perhaps Bishop Vaughan's example will move other spiritual descendants of the Apostles to venture from the cenacle to holy ground where innocent human blood is spilled in this country every twenty seconds.

What a joy if a future pastoral letter were postmarked from a jail where brother bishops are housed for justice sake! There are precedents for prison letters. There is Dr. King from a Birmingham jail, and before him Gandhi, Mindszenty, and More; before them, Peter and Paul. And there is Joan Andrews.

Some **DROPS OF LIFE** fall unobserved on the leeward side of the media's agenda, leaving us only partially informed.

How many of us have seen the following headline? "Three Catholic Nuns Jailed and Strip-Searched; Habits and Veils Confiscated. Twenty Other Women Forced to Stand Nude Before Prison Guards." Sound like El Salvador? As of this date I haven't spotted the story in newspapers, TV, or on radio; yet it happened not too long ago in swanky suburban Westchester County, New York.

If the women similarly assaulted that day had been arrested while protesting oil spills, fur coats, weaponry, apartheid, homelessness, or other safe causes, the media would have pounced on the outrage. Yet we haven't seen the headline or the story.

Could it be the women were in the wrong aisle of a pet media issue? You judge: the Sisters and eighty other women and men were sitting, praying, and blocking the entrance to an abortion clinic.

"Aaargh!" you say. "That's different!" some will say, "Women have rights to their bodies, y'know. These nuns had no business imposing their religious . . ." Suddenly, women's rights and rights to one's own body become very selectively defined, indeed.

What about the rights of women who happen also to be nuns? Or pro-life laywomen who are mothers and daughters and wives? What about their rights to their bodies? Where is the primacy of privacy we hear so often from N.O.W.? Can we expect a strident Molly Yard to castigate the people who violated the modesty of these

53

twenty-three women? Not likely. Just as you didn't see that headline.

Strip-searching nuns and other women for sitting in front of a building seems a disproportionate response. Arrest them if you must; but accord all people their rights and avoid unnecessary indignities.

To SAY, as does N.O.W., that there may be no restrictions regarding abortions is to argue like the N.R.A. Both organizations brook no limits to their license.

IS IT ODD TO FEEL perplexed that some of us who recognize abortion and euthanasia as threats to life and peace, on the one hand, continue to support a nuclear arms buildup and freer citizen access to firearms on the other? If we choose life, shouldn't we seek more consistency?

And others who speak out against nuclear proliferation and easy availability of handguns and other firearms as threats to human life seem not to consider that abortion and euthanasia are immediate and deliberate causes of death to innocents and a disruption of peace and justice in our society. We appear to fall short on reaching a consistent commitment to protect life and ensure peace.

We are a nation which in my lifetime has suffered the shooting deaths of two Kennedys, Martin Luther King, and Medgar Evers, the gunshot wounding of Ronald Reagan, the crippling of James Brady and George Wallace, and numerous injuries and deaths to innocent citizens and law-enforcement officers. Yet we put more emphasis on the right to bear arms than we do on the right to life, liberty, and the pursuit of happiness, which unfortunately are not yet explicit in our Constitution.

Weapons as diverse as nuclear bombs and small guns can be equally terminal to an individual human life. And both are threats to peace in our society.

It augurs poorly for this world if the spirit of violence captures our energy and acceptance. Forty-some years ago, Gandhi said, "Unless big nations shed their desire of exploitation and the spirit of violence, of which war is the natural expression and the atom bomb the inevitable consequence, there is no hope for peace in the world."

Shortly after, he was shot dead.

WHEN MY SON'S SORE THROAT kept him from gym class one school morning, he was officially excused for one reason: he had a note from his parents. Without this note he would not have been excused. So what succeeded in freeing this tormented teenager from an odious physical encounter was not his sore throat; it was his father's signature. Parental permission.

On those occasions when my kids did want to get athletic, the activity sponsor — school, church, community — mandated parental permission. To run cross country, to take the school ski trip, or to play Little League baseball required written approval from my wife or me.

I recall with some residual horror when a daughter persuaded us to support her adolescent need for mutilation so she could hang ornamental pendants from her ears in the manner of primitive beauties from another era. She was fourteen; I was scared. Before the jeweler could punch tiny holes in those beautiful lobes, Dad needed to sign and say it was okay. I'm still not sure it was. Her ears. My fears. Our tears. Resigned, I signed.

In those instances, society places a premium on the concern, responsibility, and authority of parents, the parent-child relationship, common sense, and just good business. A minor child is the responsibility of the parents or guardian. Almost always. And then there's abortion.

Any pregnant minor child can obtain a legal abortion from Planned Parenthood or any other state-sanctioned abortion provider without a whisper to the parents or guardian. The doctors who kill our children and grandchildren in utero operate with impunity on the bodies of young girls, also our children and grandchildren, in the name of "choice" and a good payday. Compassion of this sort comes with a fee and always at a price. It's not easy for most young girls to find $300 or the going rate to pay the physician who dismembers even the very youngest of preborn girls and boys.

But what happens if no one pays? Should parents who were not informed in advance of an elected surgical procedure be expected to pay? Chances are that decision won't come up. Abortion, unlike other operations or surgeries, is generally on a pay-first-then-be-served basis. Like at McDonald's.

It might be sadly intriguing to follow a scenario in which a minor pays for her abortion with her unknowing parents' charge card. Would they be required under law to pay? They may not wish to become accessories to a fatal act, particularly as it involves their grandchild. If they disapprove, what should be their action?

It should strike us as odd that the fragile moral gyroscope balancing contemporary American society seems to lose its coherence whenever the subject of abortion is visited.

WE YANKS ARE A STRANGE LOT. Newspaper and TV accounts range from dismay to outrage that a newborn baby, delivered by her mother in the lavatory of an airplane, was found stuffed in the trash. Thanks to God, and the plane crew, the child survives.

The resilient mother is immediately tracked down, arrested, and jailed for her action. Yet it is we who behave even more bizarrely. Consider this: instead of driving to the airport, the same woman drives to an abortion facility designed to perform late-term abortions. Tiny Elizabeth — the same child, the same age, the same day — could be aborted, likewise thrown in the trash (this time with impunity), and it is okay with the law, the media, and the citizenry of this country.

People opposing such an abortion would be branded "extreme right-wing religious fanatics." Representatives of NOW, NARAL, Planned Parenthood, the ACLU, CBS, *The New York Times*, the courts, most of Hollywood, at least one major political party, and many of the rest of us would parade righteously in favor of the mother's right under law to abort that child, Elizabeth, for whatever reason. Instead, Elizabeth lives, and we are outraged now that she was mistreated. Strange indeed.

Perhaps we accept the abortion scenario because we wouldn't have seen baby Elizabeth if terminated at nine months (or nine weeks); but when she appears at nine months we did see her. Seeing is often believing. Therefore, if I do not care to believe, I will choose not to look, lest in looking I should see. The ancient monkey at the shrine gate of Nikko obscures his sight with hand-covered eyes and sees no evil.

King Lear's Earl of Gloucester accepted the painful comfort of his own blindness because he no longer had direction, no way to follow. He stumbled when he saw, but when sighted, he also had the opportunity to adjust his vision, although he didn't.

The man born blind, on the other hand, asks only "that I may see." The beggar gives pause to his earlship.

We, too, could open our own eyes.

A MEDICAL JOURNAL REPORT detailed how British doctors performed the "first successful heart operation on a baby in its mother's womb. . ." Follow-up press items reveal also that American doctors earlier performed "the first successful operation on a fetus removed from the mother's womb and returned after life-saving lung surgery." The American operation was performed on a "twenty-four-week-old fetus" and "that baby was born three months later and is still alive six months after birth."

The journalist's use of real terms such as mother, baby, and fetus present images in contrast to today's usual euphemisms derived from an abortion mentality. Our joy at the success of these two human life-saving efforts is mitigated by confusion over society's contradictory behavior. The doctors inserted an instrument "into the heart of the *unborn baby boy*"; this is called life-saving. Yet, with allowance of our laws and current medical ethics, a doctor may yet insert an instrument into that same "unborn baby boy" to deliberately cause his death; this is called abortion.

Take a look in your phone directory yellow pages under "Clinics" and note what is advertised for other twenty-four-week-old unborn baby boys and girls. Then remember that even after twenty-four weeks a fetus/baby may be legally destroyed at your local hospital, up to the last day before birth.

What a tangled web!

THE SUCCESS OF OPERATION RESCUE points up changing realities. What pro-abortionists seem to fear is not violence, but the lack of it.

Efforts to paint pro-life people as violent just don't wash. Bombing and violence are wrong, stupid, and play into the hands of the abortion providers. The only beneficiaries of clinic bombings are the proprietors and their apologists. Insurance money, public sympathy, and obfuscation of the real violence that occurs daily within the clinics are the abortionist's payoff.

Abortion supporters reach back to the middle of the last decade to restate twenty-four claimed attacks on abortuaries (but no deaths) across the nation in one year (1984). Yet in every nine minutes of every day, twenty-four innocent preborn human lives are attacked inside the clinics. And each dies. So where is the real violence?

Biologists tell us the forty-six chromosomes that make up our own unique genetic packages are transmitted to us at conception; when else could we get twenty-three chromosomes from our dads? Our sex, race, color of eyes, and other individual traits are determined by that unique genetic recipe. Yet we are willing to scrape someone else's life package down the sewer.

Misinformation peppers the statements of many pro-abortion spokespeople — each one a former fetus. But consider this: Who is more apt to tell the truth — one who kills, or one who tries to stop the killing? Who derives economic benefit from abortion? Certainly not the pro-lifers. They do what they do for no financial gain; and it's very inconvenient, risky, and costly.

If the abortionists are committed to compassion as they say, why not do what they do for free rather than for $200 or more per hit?

Ah! But there's the rub.

SOMEONE AGAIN has asserted that, while the alarmingly high number of abortions performed in the U. S. may indicate a convenience mentality run amuck, a need for an abortion option exists to deal with the tough cases, particularly rape. The hotly disputed question of abortion finds champions lurking at both extremes. Polls continue to indicate many people find abortion distasteful but believe it ought to remain an option in cases of rape.

A civilized society must universally acknowledge that rape is a horribly brutal crime; any consideration of the victim's plight needs to be sensitive and compassionate. Any discussion of rape and abortion must not attempt to mitigate the horror a woman victim has experienced. Keeping this in mind, let's look at some arithmetic.

Government and private-sector statistics show an abortion rate of about 1.5 million souls each year; or about 4,100 abortions performed every day in this country.

FBI statistics put the number of forcible rapes at an annual rate of about 100,000. The figures on pregnancy following rape are more difficult to obtain. It may be of little consolation to recall that rape-related pregnancies are extremely rare because of trauma to the woman victim's body, a high degree of male dysfunction in the act, the age spread of victims from prepubescent to postmenopausal, use of the pill, and other factors. The few relatively current studies reported in U.S. medical journals indicate differing and inconclusive approximations of pregnancies resulting from rape. On this, however, they agree: pregnancy from rape is rare but not unknown.

Yet it is abundantly clear that the vast preponderance of abortions performed are for reasons other than rape. If as many as half of all reported rapes resulted in pregnancy followed by abortion, no more than about 100 of the 4,100 abortions performed daily could *possibly* be rape-related. Considering that not all rapes result in pregnancy, it is safe to say that of the 4,100 daily abortions, more than 4,000 are for reasons other than rape.

Well-intentioned people who feel compelled to accept the retention of all existing abortion-on-demand services because of the possibility of rape may want to think over the deaths of those four thousand other innocent babies conceived in less violent, more choice-oriented circumstances.

Perhaps those people who would allow for the deaths of the hundred (likewise innocent) who will perish today, may wish at least to step forward in defense of the four thousand freely conceived who nonetheless are also scheduled to die today. This too is a choice. Rather than silence, why not — at least in this case — choose life? Question the current law which daily permits the willful destruction of so many innocent lives, each conceived through a consensual (not forced) act. At least on this basis, join the many others concerned for the human life of both mother and child. You will find much in common. You will find that they, too, burn with compassion.

AMERICA cannot solve problems of Third World hunger and overpopulation by destroying preborn babies in American inner cities.

SOME AMERICANS BRISTLE when pro-life people compare this nation's policy on abortion with an earlier policy of slavery and with the Holocaust. Critics correctly point out that the first differs in kind from the other two. This is true; each is different. The Holocaust differs from black slavery, but who would disagree that both are wrong, both atrocities? We need not quibble over which is greater or lesser if we acknowledge they are both atrocities.

Morality notwithstanding, what is similar is the common thread tying each of the three together: the question of *legal personhood*. In each instance — slavery, genocide, and abortion — the responsible governments made a conscious decision that a group of human beings would be categorized and treated as less than human, non-persons.

Fortunately, slavery and Nazi genocide are no longer with us. Good people saw to that. Abortion, however, thrives in America as a big business of multimillion-dollar proportions. Destruction of preborn human life is the grossest of our national products.

We continue to delude ourselves. The Supreme Court did not conclude that preborn children are not human beings, only that (according to the Court) preborns are not guaranteed protection as "persons" under our Constitution.

Governments may continue to assign non-personhood to groups of humans who are at some point inconvenient. Today, it may be me; tomorrow, you. A government of, by, and for the people ought to take particular care in assuring that no human sacrifice is ever chosen or sanctioned.

68

THE **OUTRAGE EXPRESSED** by some over the use of photos showing aborted fetuses is curiously bewildering. Agreed, the content is offensive. Unfortunately, it depicts an offensive reality. Isn't the reality of that act, which destroys innocent human life, more offensive than a picture? These pictures do not promote death by abortion or any other means. Rather they make a plea for the protection of human life. Is this so offensive? Those films and photos echo the outrage of many people that these deaths are permitted to continue in a nation which purports to be concerned for human life.

I remember my horror as a child when I first viewed newsreels showing the ovens and cluttered, open graves of Hitler's death camps. Certainly these films were offensive; yet they portrayed the reality of evil to a silent world. I recall our revulsion in that instance was not directed at Paramount News for reporting the crime, but at the persons who committed the atrocities.

Although I suspect we shall continue to shoot the messenger who upsets our digestion, we might be wise to mull over the message.

THE EXECUTION OF A MAN by lethal injection
sparked a sensitive editorial by a major newspaper
supporting the medical profession's condemning as
unethical a physician's use of medical skills to cause
death.

I applaud this stance by the healing profession and the
press. The physician's role and duty are to save life, not
extinguish it. Physicians should steadfastly shun the role
of executioner. However, neither the medical profession
nor the newspaper seems particularly offended by direct
participation of physicians in administering lethal
injections to innocent preborn children in the daily
performance of abortions.

Our society has reintroduced capital punishment and
added a new killing technique to its deadly arsenal. But is
it really so new? For nearly two decades, our society has
conceded that innocent human life may be put to death by
a physician using lethal injections or other means.

It would be consistent and commendable if the
American Medical Association and major newspapers
were to speak out against lethal injections for the
innocent, as it has for those adjudged guilty.

OCCASIONALLY HEADLINES SCREAM, "Bomb Explosion Causes Damage to Abortion Clinic. . . ." Few will disagree that bombing is a terrible and wrongful response to a perceived problem.

But the wide publication of this kind of news story subtly points up the obverse: peaceful, nonviolent demonstrations are routinely ignored by the media.

Across the nation, hundreds of peaceful demonstrations — picketing and sit-in rescues — have helped to deter or postpone the deaths of innocent human lives. Often these peaceful life-saving efforts are not reported in the press — only bombings.

So long as the press is diverted by foolish bombings of the bricks and mortar outside abortion mills, it can continue to avoid reporting the destruction of human life that occurs within these clinics. And we can all blissfully ignore the painful aftermath of guilt and grief that later pursues so many frightened young women encouraged by our society to do away with their own children.

We pray there are no more bombings by misguided people. The bombers, in addition to potentially jeopardizing human lives and property, give comfort to Planned Parenthood and other abortion sponsors by playing into their deadly game of violence against innocent human life.

A **LETTER FROM A CONCERNED CATHOLIC** questioned the prudence of Father John Catoir's column "Only God Can Judge" — an open letter to those who have had abortions. The writer is disturbed by what he perceives as gratuitous forgiveness for a serious sin.

The pain is evident in the writer's message. Like others, he may feel betrayed by the Church's attentions to other sinners and what might be construed to be indifference toward loyalists. The writer has been loyal, and that is why it hurts. In the Gospel, however, an older brother, constant and faithful, is hurt and confused when the father extends love, forgiveness, and even celebration to his alienated son.

Christ gives the same message again in the person of the shepherd who rejoices over finding the one lost sheep. Yet he doesn't love the ninety-nine any less. He knows he can depend on them to follow him.

The father of the prodigal needed the older son's support. In his long-awaited moment, the father was robbed of joy by the older son's complaint and unwillingness to share in the family reunion. The unfortunate father again lost one son by reclaiming the other. He just couldn't win!

Father Catoir, by reaching out to those taken in abortion, is moved with the compassion of a loving pastor, or father, or shepherd. Father Catoir is simply living the Gospel. He is, after all, not condoning abortion, the sin. Rather, he is saying that God loves the sinner, and particularly the sinner who repents. And in abortion, the woman is a victim as well as the child. As a counselor,

Father Catoir is sensitive to the anguish and remorse of many who have had abortions. We should not condemn the woman after an abortion. What end, what good would it accomplish? We should rather try to educate, persuade or prevent it beforehand, and offer alternatives, such as adoption.

Like Father Catoir, we must love the victims — woman and child (yes, and even the abortionist) — if we are to be worthy of the name Christian.

Some of the truest supporters of life are the courageous women of WEBA — Women Exploited by Abortion — and AVA — American Victims of Abortion. These are women who in the past have undergone abortions, some more than once. In time, most suffered great guilt and sorrow. Yet through loving support from people like Father Catoir and mutual sharing with one another, they now publicly make the most moving, personalized arguments against the evils of abortion. They have been there and seen the ugliness.

And they have been welcomed back by a loving heavenly Father, who opens his arms and rejoices that his daughters who were lost are found.

FORTY DAYS AFTER his arrest for the defense of preborn human life, a seventy-two-year-old retired Catholic priest was led out of an Atlanta prison into the soft daylight rain. Forty days of prayer and fasting and reparation. Forty days in the desert of an American prison. Forty days in which one hundred sixty thousand preborn American innocents joined the hosts of heaven.

Operation Rescue continues as other seasoned rescuers are led from Georgia jails. More rescues, packaged and imported from the lessons of Atlanta, are being staged in New Jersey, Illinois, Louisiana, Pennsylvania, New England, New York, California, Ohio, Michigan, Maryland, Washington, D.C., and elsewhere by people trained in the jails of Atlanta.

In time, the main body of rescuers will be gone with the wind from Atlanta. Perhaps that wind, like the breeze which quickened the Apostles in the upper room, will release a Spirit over America that results in no more killing of preborn children, or damaged and handicapped babies, or the elderly ill, or the outcast and unwanted.

Then the prison yard of Atlanta will be called holy ground.

PLANNED PARENTHOOD'S INFATUATION
WITH THE CONDOM CULTURE knows neither
seasonal nor tasteful bounds. Or at least appearances so
indicate.

This past Christmas, the PP franchise in Paterson, N.J.,
featured in its display window a Christmas tree adorned
with colorfully tinseled condoms. This appears to be the
organization's way to welcome and celebrate the birth of
the Child who, for Christians over the centuries, is
recognized as the Savior of the world. When faced with
criticism from offended Christians, a PP spokeswoman
offered that "it is not unusual for organizations to include
customized decorations that are a theme." Some theme!

While other Paterson windows display a Santa or
Nativity scene, PP somehow finds in Christmas, as it does
in all things, an opportunity to peddle its sex-as-a-game
message.

Perhaps by defacing the arboreal symbol of Christmas,
the nation's largest purveyor of abortion subtly expresses
its disapproval of the birth two thousand years ago of a
child to a poor, unwed teenage mother. How anathema
the circumstances of that first Christmas must seem to the
enemies of childbirth. And how predictable that the
condom tree received outspoken support from a Passaic
clergyman who also sits in the president's chair of that
county's PP Board of Directors.

It's probable that on Christmas day this minister of
God, like so many other clergymen, reminded his
congregation that the birth of the poor child in a
Bethlehem hovel foretold hope and good news for the

world. And perhaps the minister also recalled the young, innocent children slaughtered days later to rid the world of that baby whom Herod felt would threaten his own kingly lifestyle.

Although this minister may misguidedly side with today's Herodians, he at least stands up publicly for a position on abortion. Too many other clergymen, it appears, fail to speak out against what their hearts and minds and theology tell them is wrong. These are those who, when pressed in private, nervously acknowledge the error of abortion; but in public, and in the pulpit, they look away in silence as Herod's troops ride through the streets, innocent blood dripping from politically correct swords.

REMEMBRANCE OF THE NAZI
HOLOCAUST of the 1940s remains very much in the news today. After the horrors of the Holocaust, people asked, "How could this happen?" There were no good answers. Only this: because we let it happen. And that's true today with our own American silent holocaust of the innocent preborn, and perhaps soon our sick and elderly and handicapped.

If we don't stand up now and say, "No, enough killing," we will again allow a holocaust to continue.

I recently re-viewed the 1950s film "Judgment at Nuremberg" — a grim depiction of the Nazi war criminal trials after World War II. Some of the statements from that old film are hauntingly prophetic of today. For example: "Others must share in the guilt of what happens!" and "Where were we when children were being carried off to their executions?"

Where are we, indeed?

IN THE SUMMER OF THE YEAR MADE
FAMILY BY GEORGE ORWELL, six out-of-state
protestors, four women and two men, stood before a
judge of the Sixth District Court of Maryland, at
Gaithersburg. The charge was "loitering" in front of an
abortion facility; the proscribed action had taken the form
of a nonviolent sit-in which shut down the facility,
resulting in no deaths that day at that place. At least one
client changed her mind and went instead to a crisis
pregnancy center where new life-giving options were
offered and accepted.

An hour or so before the Gaithersburg trial began, the
judge called the six before him and warned that he would
allow no testimony involving religion, God, killing, or
anything external to the actual charge of loitering,
including the motive. If the word "abortion were simply
uttered, challenged the judge, the gavel would slam down
and the violator would be charged with contempt of court.

The defendants acted as their own lawyers (*pro se*)
despite the tired bromide about fools for clients. The six
committed to identify with the unborn who have no
defense. Nan Elliott and Mary Kay Stine had come from
Virginia, Joan Andrews from Delaware, Tom Herlihy
from New York, Mary Foley and one other from New
Jersey.

When it was time for an opening statement, the six,
aware of the judicial threat concerning abortion, held that
word until last. They said, in part: ". . . we seek only that
each living human being be assured of that same right
which we here all have: that is, to continue uninterrupted

by outside force, that life which is already begun. . . . We simply attempted to save innocent young lives from immediate danger of death, and young women from possible injury and exploitation by abortion."

But in fact they were hamstrung at every turn within that courtroom. The abortionist from the struck facility presented himself as a witness and was subsequently picked apart in cross examination by each of the six defendants. Throughout, the judge raised obstacles and blocked necessary language and references by the defendants.

In time, each was found guilty. The judge began to pronounce sentence: "Let me say this to you before I give you an opportunity to speak. You may tell me anything you'd like about your background, where you work, your family, or your past record. You will not tell me about your personal beliefs as to why you did this. It is of no moment as to why you did this. Nor anything about the cause for which you were found guilty. Do you have any questions?"

A young lawyer observing from the rear of the courtroom approached the bench. The lawyer, not representing or known by the defendants before that day, spoke out: ". . . I'm not concerned about the cause, your honor. I am concerned about the fact, and certainly we have all read the opinions of the court of appeals. The court of appeals has been absolutely clear. It said an individual has an absolute right to bring to the judge anything that the individual believes could mitigate sentence. I understand, your honor, that you may have heard what these people have to say before; but I think they have a right under our Constitution to say it, and I would ask you to give that serious consideration."

"Wow!" thought one of the defendants. "This must be James Madison . . . or John Wayne." It wasn't; he was simply an attorney with a passion for constitutional justice, the cause notwithstanding. And his self-initiated action provided each of the Gaithersburg six and opportunity to speak for life. And what a happy opportunity it was. Reluctantly allowed five minutes each, a total of thirty minutes, the six under the guilty verdict spoke for nearly two hours. The exercise proved powerful. All parties were emotionally wrung out by the varied yet life-focused testimony of the six. People in the seats wept. Even the judge's eyes misted over at several points. Truth can be terribly potent when spoken from the heart and without rancor by people of unyielding decency even under a yoke of impending punishment.

By the end of the day, the heart of the judge, who had so forcefully denied the defendants any free-speech reference to the motive which led to the trial, was visibly softened. Nan Elliott spoke of her hope that had she been in Germany in the 1940s or in the American South in the 1960s, she would have done something. "I cannot," she said, "stand by and watch a human being die and do nothing."

The judge broke his silence: "Mrs. Elliott, let me say this. When we stop having people like you who espouse their causes in the United States, we're going to be in big trouble."

Finally, sentenced to pay a fine their consciences would not permit, the defendants were remanded to jail. As the marshals of the court came forward to manacle the hands of the guilty, the judge commanded, "Don't handcuff these people. They'll leave with their dignity." The courtroom erupted in applause.

A minor case. A simple sentence of several days to be served. Yet the defendants experienced immersion in a selfless appeal for justice on behalf of others unnamed, unborn, who were not there that day and might never see the light of any day.

However, events within that courtroom would have been quite different except for a young attorney who happened to be in court on other business that morning.

Thanks go to that man from Maryland, and to those other attorneys who continue to step forward in *pro bono* generosity to bring the full expression of constitutional rights to average persons who, through the prejudice of a judge, might be denied what is theirs as full citizens of this nation.

YOUR HONOR, we stand before this court, all loyal citizens of the United States. Individually, we are teachers, business men and women, housewives and professionals. We have served this nation in Vietnam and in other government service. We work with children and with the poor. We labor in the offices and yards of American industry. We tend our homes and our families.

Collectively, we are charged with purposeless assembly. We intend to demonstrate that our peaceful activity was indeed purposeful and, to our minds, legal. And we propose to show that we acted from compelling motives. For we do no one harm. We wish no one ill. We commit no violence. Rather we seek only that each living human being be assured of that same right which we here all have: that is, to continue, uninterrupted by outside force, that life which is already begun.

Specifically, we simply attempted to save innocent young lives from immediate danger of death, and young women from possible injury and exploitation by abortion.

[Opening defense statement in a Maryland trial of six out-of-state residents for loitering at a Gaithersburg abortion center, 1984]

WHILE THUMBING THROUGH THE
DIOCESAN NEWSPAPER, I happily came upon an
article about a friend who puts her pro-life work where
her heart is. Kathy DiFiore, founder of Several Sources
Foundation, long ago opened her home and her heart to
young women with crisis pregnancies. In some ways,
Kathy's gift offers new insights into the Christmas story.

Although only recently discovered by the media,
Kathy and her small dedicated staff have for years quietly
made room at the inn of compassion to shelter and
counsel troubled young women. Kathy and company
have given support which continues to save lives.

Why a Christmas insight? At that Nativity we think of
the joy of Mary and the Christ Child. But we need also to
recall that the unwed, teenage Mary was pregnant and
had only her faith in God to sustain her.

She needed support and found it in Joseph, who by the
circumstances and law of the day could have denounced
her and walked away. Joseph had a choice provided by
law; yet Joseph chose life. It was not his child, as these
are not Kathy's children.

But both people, through love, provided a young
mother the support systems needed to cope. One shudders
to consider how today's forces of convenience would
advise the unwed, pregnant, teenaged Mary. Thank God
for Joseph. Thank God for Kathy DiFiore and others,
known and unknown, who do what she does.

The work is God's work: the work of Kathy and
Several Sources, Birthright, crisis pregnancy centers, and
people who open their homes to frightened, troubled
young women. And it is God's work that others, too,

strive unceasingly through peaceful means to save the two victims present at each abortion.

It is God's work, true; but it is also Joseph's human role and example to us. He was made for more than standing unnoticed in the shadows of a crèche. And this is the Christmas insight: we are all called like Joseph to be a support to the troubled.

But what if there were no Joseph? Or today, no Kathy DiFiores? Would we stand by as the pregnant teenager is advised and encouraged to abort?

Christ says what we have done to the least we have done to Him, and we will be judged by what we have done. Perhaps we need to ask: What are we doing to Him?

EACH DAY PRO-LIFE PEOPLE PICKET along sidewalks leading to abortion clinics and hospitals throughout the country. Their presence is irritating to some and reassuring to others. The purpose of these peaceful demonstrations is to call attention to the legalized elimination of innocent life, known as "choice."

People carrying placards and offering counsel for alternatives to abortion give witness to their belief that each human life is unique, individual, and sacred. Yet even as the picketing continues, the deaths mount.

The picketing is important because there are people standing outside our modern death camps who will not be silent. At some future Nuremberg it may be said that some Americans believed the taking of innocent human life was wrong, despite a Supreme Court ruling that it is okay to kill so long as s/he, like Dred Scott, is not a "person in the sense of the Constitution."

What is needed to save lives? Southern lunch counters were not integrated because of pickets and placards and letters to the editor. It wasn't the cries of dissenters that opened the front of the bus to American blacks, or gave nationhood to India. Our own history has shown that where all else failed, nonviolent direct action often achieved the goal.

But there are some personal risks to this. Please God, there may be even more people who will take the risk to rescue the innocent and combat the violence of abortion through nonviolent direct action employing Gandhian principles as lovingly and successfully as did Dr. Martin Luther King, Jr.

All we are asking is give life a chance.

A RECENT ITEM DISMISSING PRO-LIFE
BELIEF as a male-dominated conspiracy brings to
mind Oscar Wilde's quip that nothing succeeds like
excess.

While recalling accurately that a man once asked
former President Reagan to pardon someone jailed for
knocking down the bricks and mortar of an abortion
chamber, the writer implicitly tries to link that male
request with the leadership of the January March for
Life. She is misinformed. The founder, leader, and
spokesperson of the annual March for Life is Nellie
Gray, a Washington attorney, but a woman first. Her
assistant for operations has been Dee Becker, also a
woman. Women are clearly the leaders of the march.

But the writer is further alarmed that the executive
director of a local crisis pregnancy center is male. Did she
miss the irony that the executive director of the local
Planned Parenthood is also male?

The writer does make a valid point when she suggests
that, to be consistent, Catholic bishops should consider
excommunicating Catholic male doctors who perform
abortions. Perhaps all Catholic bishops ought to
investigate this course. Clearly, some already have done
so. To say a Catholic doctor who knowingly and willfully
continues to destroy innocent human lives on demand is
truly Catholic is as absurd as saying that Nazi doctor
Josef Mengele was truly a Christian. Of course, history
bears out that the American abortionist doctor and the
Nazi exterminator doctor worked within the laws of their
respective societies. A thought for the writer to reflect on

is that, like Mengele, most American abortionists are male.

These male abortionists are getting rich in the multimillion-dollar abortion industry; that's what should put a chill in the writer. These men daily perform thousands of rape-like abortion procedures on young women with crisis pregnancies. It isn't the pro-life males or counselors at the crisis pregnancy center who invade the bodies of young women to destroy human life in utero and possibly endanger the women's health.

Perhaps the real perpetrators — the abortionists — are the males with whom women should be angry. Isn't it the male abortionist who collects lucrative fees at the expense of the female's dignity and the young life within her uterus?

According to biology, the sex of the child is determined at conception by the combination of chromosomes (XX=female; XY=male). Since XX is the predominant combination, it could be argued that most aborted babies are female.

Who will weep for their women's rights?

SHORTLY AFTER HOLY INNOCENTS DAY, about three-dozen clergy published a plea to Morris County (N.J.) freeholders to revisit rejected public funding of Planned Parenthood (PP). When that many clergypersons write as clergy and not simply as persons, I'm led to conclude they are making a religious statement. And that's okay.

But when a clergy group united for defense of PP upbraids the results of a democratic balloting process exercised by our elected officials, I'm inclined to twitch a bit.

Planned Parenthood of America, of which the Morristown-Dover unit is essentially a franchise, provides and promotes abortion services. So far as I know, the local PP does not directly commit abortions; it directly refers clients to those who will. But if one takes the family name in hope of the high road, one likewise can expect to share in the road's mud and furrows. In this, the local unit is inextricably bound to the PP family name.

PP falls short on consistency in voicing concern for prenatal care. How can a participant in the abortion of prenatals be taken seriously about its claimed concern for prenatals? Prenatal vacuuming of the uterus and saline injections can play nasty havoc with prenatal as well as maternal health.

We've all heard it: when a provider participates in abortion of a prenatal, the act is euphemistically labeled "termination of a pregnancy" or "removal of fetal tissue." When that same provider opts not to abort the prenatal, it's called concern for "babies at risk" of prenatal or perinatal death.

How can prenatal deaths be a serious concern to the abortion provider when prenatal death is the very definition of abortion?

More doublespeak from double-P.

WE SPEAK GLIBLY OF RIGHT TO LIFE; we need also to write for and about that life to our state and federal representatives, and to our neighbors through the press. This is how the unempowered Every person in our society may gain the ear of those decision makers and uncommitted voters around us.

Letters carry our opinions directly (sort of) to office holders on local committees, county freeholds, state assemblies and senates, and the federal congress concerning the appropriations and expenditures of tax monies and voting directions. Our words may be handwritten or typed. Avoid form letters; write your own version, no matter how short in length. Your aim is to communicate and instruct your representative to vote in support of human life. People should not feel that their writing lacks persuasion so long as it carries conviction. Often politicians count only the ayes and nays of constituents with little attention to the specific words. That's unfortunate, perhaps, but a fact in the lives of busy office holders. Politicians pay most attention to their own voting constituencies for obvious reasons.

It's not hyperbole to assert that the media are notoriously "pro-choice." Yet while the citizen is often essentially locked out from voicing a position that commands front-page attention, most newspapers do provide an opinion page for readers to freely express opinions. Letters to the editor may not seem an exciting or profitable pursuit, but studies have shown they are read and can have an influence on the reader's awareness of the abortion madness.

It is important to keep pro-life messages before the public if we are ever to change hearts and conquer public apathy. Our thoughtful letters can emerge as powerful essays in support of life issues. And if pro-lifers won't make use of the op/ed page, we can be sure the pro-abortion columnists and apologists will.

To my mind, letters to pro-life publications are good, but often the impact is misplaced. It's an example of us talking to ourselves. Consider: We are each already committed to fight the evils of abortion, infanticide, and euthanasia; so why spend so much in effort and stamps reviewing with one another what we already clearly believe?

What is needed is to put our principles and positions in the press that is read by those who disagree with us, or who may not have any formulated opinion on abortion and other life issues. We need to seed the secular press; but we can and should continue to include correspondence to church, diocesan, and other religious publications.

Experts in persuasion advise that we reach people in terms of their own values. If our readership or audience is secular, nonreligious, or non-Christian, it makes little practical sense and will bear no fruit if we start preaching Christianity as the reason why our readers should be persuaded to embrace our opposition to abortion.

If your audience is the readership of a church-, mosque-, or orthodox synagogue-oriented publication, then religious and scriptural references can be fruitful.

Tailor your letters to fit the intended audience. Remember, the intent is to make the reader think without getting angry at you, the writer. You want him/her to get angry with the 4,200 abortions committed every day in this country. You want to present, enlighten, persuade, and direct the reader to a knowledge of what is really happening in our societal binge against human life.

It's a good idea to learn in advance the guidelines for submitting a letter to a particular paper. A safe bet may be to make your letter no longer than one double-spaced, typewritten page (8½ x 11 inches). However, a call to the editor of the opinion/editorial page will ensure that you get the specific requirements for that newspaper. Most letters-to-the-editor pages limit the length of submissions to a given number of words. If the writer is verbose, the letter is unlikely to see printer's ink.

Your letter will be more effective if it's simple and focused. Limit your letter to one specific theme. Avoid the scatter-gun approach which attempts to cram in all possible argumentation for and against this and that. If, for example, you're writing about teenage parental consent, stick to that topic and make one or two good points; that's all the reader needs or wants. You can cover another anti-abortion specific next time. Newspaper readers quickly move off the overly comprehensive missive. A good pro-life letter is meant to be instructive to the reader and not a cathartic exercise for the writer.

Make sure you include your name, and give your address and a phone where you can be reached. This is important to the newspaper if they wish to verify that you indeed are the author.

Be positive and good-humored, or at least composed. Avoid anger, preaching, and name-calling; it will backfire. What you have on your side is truth. That ought to set you free. Truth, using the scientific facts surrounding the development of human life and the consequences of abortion, is your long suit. Use it wisely.

92

Make it clear that your concern is for more than the child. We are too often criticized (unfairly, I believe) for lacking compassion for the frightened woman who is caught in a crisis pregnancy. She too is a victim. We must be open to her, to support her and provide her with alternatives to abortion. Our letter should convey this. Said one group of American bishops: "Our concern for the life of unborn children must be matched by our sensitivity and love for women with unexpected or problem pregnancies."

Finally, you must sign the letter. This, as with a daytime phone number, is for the newspaper's and your protection.

Then like a good scout, be prepared. You may see your published letter edited, words or sentences cut out without benefit of a smooth transition, and perhaps even inaccurate changes made to your fine prose. But that's a small fee exacted for your courageous stand for human life. You will know that you stood up and spoke out, and that others heard.

It takes some courage for anyone to write his/her local newspaper. You put your name and the beliefs of your heart before the eyes of your neighbors who may disagree with you. But that's their problem. Our job resides in educating the uncommitted by presenting the information needed to change hearts.

Derek Bok, as president of Harvard, said, "If you think education is expensive, try ignorance." And that's our challenge. We must live by and teach the sanctity of all human life to an increasingly hardened society. Not to do so now would indeed add to the great cost already borne by our troubled nation.

AN APOCRYPHAL MATRON named Sweeney, it is rumored, suggests that January 22 be designated as National Fetal Neglect Day, featuring a one-day moratorium on societally imposed guilt. The intent of this nationwide hands-off day is to free any pregnant woman to exercise for twenty-four hours a right to choose whatever she likes regarding her own pregnancy.

Among the menu of choices, Ms. Sweeney advocates that any pregnant woman who damn-well-feels-like-it light up a pack of her favorite cigarettes and puff the smoke in the direction of the Surgeon General of her choice.

Similar encouragements extend to proscribed alcohol use and — with discretion based on local penal code — the use of drugs.

The author of National Fetal Neglect Day strongly recommends that gravid participants limit chosen abuse to one day. Unless of course, they plan to abort. In that case smoking, drinking, and drug damage to the fetus won't matter. The little dickens will never know.

I suspect the busybodies in this country might find objection in that too.

A **POPULAR OPINION CIRCULATES** that abortion is "a Catholic issue." Perhaps the public has been nurtured on this opprobrium by pro-abortion-choice propagandists. The tactic distracts one from the issue in point and plays instead to Catholic-bashing and base bigotry which is always in season. And clearly it works.

But pro-life Protestants, Evangelicals, Greek Orthodox, Mormons, Muslims and Orthodox Jews know that the Catholic angle is just so much baloney. The Catholic label misleads because many other religious congregations likewise reject abortion on demand as evil. And fancy this: Acknowledged atheists, such as Nat Hentoff of *The Village Voice*, are outspoken in their condemnation of abortion on demand.

Catholics may wonder why the media fail to clarify that solidarity-of-belief position to the public more effectively. My suspicion is that leaders of other pro-life religious and non-religious groups genuinely try but are just not catching a sympathetic journalist's ear. And they can't feel very secure being labeled as Catholic dogmatists. Some may even be jumping up and down, waving Psalters at the media and me-too yelling, "Hey! Over here! We oppose abortion, too." But the media are often tone deaf; they appear to believe that everyone actively opposing abortion is an agent of Rome.

Today, Evangelical Christians are in the forefront of the fight against the taking of preborn innocent human life. Other groups such as the Protestant Christian Action Council, and Rabbis Against Abortion led by Rabbi Yehuda Levin, remain publicly faithful to the cause of life. Is it the American way to label these good people as Catholics? That might appear to be as oxymoronic as calling Ted Kennedy devout.

As a pressure release, some people in our society may think it healthy to select groups on whom others may vent their politically correct spleen. Some groups which may be verbally assaulted with impunity include skinheads, Communists (although they are enjoying a benign comeback lately), racists, and ax murderers. Add Roman Catholics to that list, too.

New York's liberal Senator Moynihan puzzles over why so many liberals talk tolerance and righteously oppose bigotry except in the case of this one religious group. But who can figure liberals?

It might signal good fellowship next Lenten season if another religious group stepped forward as sort of a designated hittee to take some of the heat and dog-doo off Catholics who already wear ashes to inaugurate the lean days of Lent.

After Easter, we'll be prepared to take it on again.

A **YOUNG LETTER WRITER RAILED** that pro-lifers "kill . . . and beat people" who disagree with them. Rather intemperate speech that is also false and cruelly irresponsible. On the contrary, it is the incessant daily killing by abortion that spurs pro-lifers to speak out against organized death dealing.

Can the writer flesh out her allegations and reveal the name of a person killed by a pro-life person or organization? Not likely. While she might be impressed by the names of those killed by abortionists, we may presume that the twenty-eight million legally aborted preborns were denied names as well as life. But names are freely available of the scores of young women who died following "safe" legal abortions in authorized clinics. The relocation of a practitioner's shingle from the shadows of a back alley to the sunlight of the front porch doesn't guarantee against injury or death from the abortionist's arsenal.

Now the writer wants to take us for a "walk through the streets of Newark . . ." so we may see "the quality of life facing the poor." What does this mean, vis-à-vis abortion? Is she saying that poor children who will grow to poor adulthood would be better off dead?

Some of us in walking the streets of Newark each week do see and feed the poor of all ages. And while their station may be low, their spirit is so often higher than those who wish them ill or deprive them of a shot at life, "quality" notwithstanding.

"Let them open their homes and hearts to those in need," she continues. Agreed. A good course for everyone. Perhaps an audit should be made — as one day it will — of those who do support others in need: the poor, the troubled, the AIDS victim, the disabled, developmentally impaired, the homeless, the woman with a crisis pregnancy, the threatened unborn child struggling for life in the danger zone of a mother's womb. My observation finds that pro-life people stand well represented among those who open home, heart, and pocketbook.

WHEN DOES HUMAN LIFE BEGIN? I used to think it began on Friday at five. Now, looking back presents a clearer view than when I looked ahead.

I am a middle-aged man who seems to recall having been a young man. Before that I was an adolescent. Before that, a child. Before that I was a fetus. But before that, an embryo. Before that, biologists say, I was a zygote ("Zy got rhythm! Zy got music. . ."). And before that, I was not.

Pushing my religion on someone? Not at all. Ministers and priests and rabbis aren't into zygotes. But biological science is ("who could ask for anything more!").

IN THE ACTS OF THE APOSTLES, Luke recounts how lawful authorities arrested and reproached Peter and John for teaching in the name of Jesus. The Apostles responded, "You must judge whether in God's eyes it is right to listen to you and not to God. We cannot promise to stop proclaiming what we have seen and what we have heard. . . . Obedience to God comes before obedience to man" (Acts 4:19-20, 5:29).

In the intervening two millennia, successors to those Apostles have not always spoken out so courageously concerning the primacy of God's law over man's.

But beneath the trees in the center of Morristown the day before Mother's Day, Bishop Frank Rodimer spoke out publicly and eloquently, stressing Christ's message of peace and the essential sanctity of human life from conception to natural death.

The bishop spoke under a cloudless sky before several hundred people of different faiths who are concerned with the sanctioned societal violence of our age. He repudiated abortion, euthanasia, apartheid, discrimination, and the neglect of the poor. And he spoke of peace.

His was truly an all-encompassing pro-life message, and his presence energized a long-faithful laity who sometimes teeter on the edge of hopelessness.

It should be said that the bishop was fully scheduled that Saturday morning and was en route to participate in a college graduation program. Yet Bishop Rodimer found the time to speak out for Christ in His distressing disguise of the endangered preborn.

There were other fine speakers and witnesses, such as

Olivia Gans, who shared her pain of loss as a victim undergoing an abortion; and Delores Grier, who sees the scars of abortion in her Harlem community. And there was Candy Valvano, who planned and organized this beautiful celebration of life.

But the active participation of a courageous Catholic prelate like Bishop Rodimer provides the kind of leadership, encouragement, and hope that had been long missing from our pro-life ministry.

Some pro-life people express disappointment with many of our clergy on the issue of activism for life. Priests, ministers, rabbis, and other religious often seem conspicuously absent from risk encounters that characterized the heroes of Acts. It's been said that some of the clergy seem still to be huddled in that locked upper room waiting for the Holy Spirit to arrive with the gift of fortitude.

Perhaps the emerging strong leadership of our U.S. bishops on life, peace, and poverty will strengthen and inspire us all — religious and laity.

At the Crucifixion, only the beloved disciple and a trio of Marys (always the women!) remained publicly at the foot of the cross to witness to Christ's death. It was inspiring on that Morristown green to see one of John's apostolic successors stand publicly with three contemporary women to give witness to Christ's life.

A *U.S. NEWS & WORLD REPORT* **ARTICLE** on prenatal (preborn) testing opens: "The earlier a problem pregnancy can be identified, the sooner a couple can opt for an abortion. . . ." Among the problems cited for which abortion seems an "opt-able" solution is "the risk of carrying a child with Down Syndrome. . . ." What does this say about our societal attitude toward those with Down Syndrome? What does this say to those who have forms of mental retardation? Perhaps it says: you are a problem and could have been aborted; then you wouldn't be here to cause us perfect people this problem.

Clearly, retardation in a child is a problem for parents and for society. And so are a child's involvement in an auto accident, drug use, or even a life of petty crime. Yet we don't terminate life at any stage for these problems. Nor, God forbid, should we.

But we are willing and able to opt to rip apart tiny bodies because it is projected that their mental development may not be so rapid as the norm. Most people, I believe, would recoil from the suggestion that we terminate at some level of development those among us who are labeled Down-Syndrome or retarded. Why would we knowingly allow destruction of these born or preborn children whom we would later support and cheer in Special Olympics? Perhaps we think if we destroy them, sooner, rather than later, it won't bother us so much because we won't have seen them. Yet if life is a continuum, the preborn little girl is the same individual who will later become a woman. If we kill the child, we've killed the woman.

There are better ways to greet the handicapped. Organizations such as the Association for Retarded Citizens (ARC) devote untold hours, energy, and love to enrich the lives of those of us born with any degree of retardation. ARC members and volunteers speak joyfully of how their own lives have been brightened by neighbors labeled retarded. Retarded citizens live in our communities, perform productive jobs, and bring unending good cheer to our neighborhoods. Down-Syndrome people are generally love-bringers who commit no evil and are never mean-spirited; they ask only for acceptance and an occasional hug.

Why do we view their early deaths as a reasonable option? If we can freely dispatch our preborn child now, what assurances do we have that our born Down-Syndrome child will not be terminated later, as a teenager or adult? Selective termination was opted in enlightened Europe in the 1920s and perfected there in the 1940s. Now it happens here.

And what of the distressed woman within whose womb lives a fetus (child) diagnosed to have Down Syndrome? We ought to extend to her (and the often-forgotten father, grandparents, and siblings) the fullness of life-giving counsel and support prenatally, through birth, and throughout life. There are many ways to do this: through active understanding of the family; support of mental retardation societies; ethical research; and by volunteering time and aid.

It's our society, and as John Donne pointed out, each one's death diminishes us all. It's all the more tragic when we freely opt to add to our own diminishment.

BLACKSTONE'S EPIGRAM that it is better for ten guilty to escape than that one innocent be punished has a nice ring to it. Yet today, many who would support that maxim for the primacy of innocence also hold tight to the somewhat antithetical Blackmun's "enigmagram." The Blackmun solution goes something like: it is better that any number of innocent be punished ("terminated") than for one "unwanted" to be born.

With the emergence of the science of fetology and real-time sonogram, the judicial travesty of Roe v. Wade just doesn't wash. The lives destroyed in two decades of choice remain innocent.

Most who support abortion as an option no longer deny that life exists in the uterus. The more recent shift to a quality-of-life rationale likewise fails to taint the innocence of the victims. Some well-meaning pro-choice people now say they regret the loss of the child's life but feel they must choose in favor of the mother. Yet that argument concerning a choice between lives is relevant only in a life-threatening abortion situation. The overwhelming majority of abortions are freely chosen as a backup for contraception.

The option is open to save both lives. Concern for both woman and child has spurred establishment of crisis pregnancy centers throughout the country. Here a woman finds true options that don't result in anyone's death. There are no fees. There is support throughout pregnancy and beyond, and help to choose whether to keep or place the baby with loving adoptive parents.

OUR DIOCESAN JUSTICE AND PEACE COMMISSION sensed some value in encouraging a personal presence at the March for the Homeless in our Nation's Capital. And they walked their talk. Like single candles, each one who marched gave off a small spark of awareness to this national problem. Yet with the combined light of thousands of others, each became a part of a luminous body which can impact on both congress and presidential cabinet. Or so the papers say.

Some believe that direct action accomplishes little. That's often the result. But aren't we as Christians and Jews called to do something? Called to give witness to something? If, for example, we know hungry people are in our midst, do we not have a compelling need to act? If we know innocent human lives are being put to death in our communities, ought we not at least to do something?

In one sermon on Respect Life Sunday, a priest confessed he personally saw no value in marches and rallies. That's okay. But in so saying, he may have eased certain residual twinges we parishioners suffer when we know we ought to be doing something and are not. Yet he was quite prophetic. On the previous day, a rally for life took place in the state capital. For three weeks the planned rally was announced in the bulletin, and parishioners were invited to participate. On the day of the rally only three people of my parish made the short trip by car. And perhaps only three felt an ache that next day, when it issued from the altar that marches aren't really of much value or necessarily the best approach. I don't disagree entirely with that; but I would like to have heard a specific suggestion as to what would be an effective approach. It may be that marches and rallies in support of a cause are of little consequence. Fortunately, not everyone has learned that.

The drafters of our Bill of Rights were aware of the potential expressive power that comes from peaceful assembly. If participating in rallies, marches, and nonviolent demonstrations bears little success, let's not tell the heirs of Dr. King or Mahatma Gandhi. It wasn't people who stayed at home that integrated lunch counters of the South; it wasn't Don't-Get-Involved that won statehood for India. It wasn't avoidance of thorny issues that prompted a visit to Pharaoh by an Egyptian Jew who demanded that his people be let go; or that led a radical, itinerant Rabbi and His companions to Jerusalem a week before the first Easter.

Several years ago, before Operation Rescue was born, I shared with Mother Teresa my concern over an upcoming trial resulting from a peaceful, nonviolent action at an abortuary. I told her what I had done and why. She tapped on my forehead with her index finger and said, "Keep at it."

We are all called to keep at it when justice needs serving for the hungry, the homeless, handicapped, preborn, elderly ill, each other, and for Him who appears in whatever least disguise.

Giving PUBLIC MONEY FOR PRENATAL CARE to Planned Parenthood, the nation's largest provider of abortions, makes as much sense as awarding a transportation grant to Mussolini because fascist regimes assure that trains run on time.

To say that money given to an abortion provider will not be used for prenatal abortion but for prenatal care raises this current theater beyond the absurd. For example, if you support my choice to smoke or not smoke tobacco and then give me ten dollars so long as I don't use that ten for cigarettes: I, if a smoker, can put your ten in my health account, move another ten over to my tobacco account, and buy cigarettes from the second account. What have you done? You've empowered me to feed my smoking habit although you claim your gift was not used for cigarettes. Then if you give me thousands of dollars, I can buy, not only cigarettes, but also stock in the tobacco companies fouling up the lungs of your own young children.

One cannot remain silent on this. If my money is used to spill innocent human blood, that blood is on my hands as well. Executions of innocents, legal or otherwise, cannot be justified by any honest, clear-thinking American. But clear thinking is a casualty of the abortion-on-demand debate. Some will claim that abortion is needed to help a parent-to-be. This is a massive obfuscation and does long-term disservice to a pregnant woman, not to mention what it does to her former child. One cannot help a parent by killing a child.

A different, more civilized approach is needed. The protection, provision, and support of life-giving alternatives to women caught in an unwanted or crisis pregnancy must be promulgated and supported. A mother should not be encouraged to participate in the death of her own child. Funding support for pregnant women and their prenatal children should be given to women through life-givers, not life-takers; to Birthright or other vital organizations, not Planned Parenthood.

We cannot allow those who profit from the heinous abortion industry to hoodwink us into thinking they are anointed to protect the lives of our innocent prenatals. One cannot say the fox will safeguard the chickens when he has feathers in his teeth and, literally, egg on his face.

We cannot be silent on this legalized criminality of our time. Listen up, America: 4,200 prenatal children died from abortion on demand today! That's the same number of prenatals who died yesterday. Want tomorrow's count? Or can we all project from today what has happened every day since early 1973? It will continue into the future until we say: hold, enough!

We are all here for a while, then we are gone. If we die from natural causes, we expire analogously to a fetus who succumbs to nature's spontaneous aborting by miscarriage. If we die at the hands of another, it is analogous to man-caused abortion, which Hippocrates admonished all physicians never to do. But the miscarriage in this second analogy involves justice, or rather its violation, and is not an inexplicable act of nature. And we are responsible for our acts, not nature's.

But whether I am aborted in this final trimester of my

life by nature or by man, I will until that moment join others who point out the nakedness of the Gray Emperor of Abortion, whatever his loyal subjects deign to view through stained gauze darkly.

WHILE **CHRISTOPHER COLUMBUS** celebrated in the limelight of his most significant find, another Italian was turning the city of Florence on its ear by the heat of his spirited preaching against the climate of moral laxity. Girolamo Savonarola, Dominican preacher and reformer, railed against the seduction by greed, vanity, and pleasure in the lives of some of his more powerful neighbors — including a Pope — and placed his future on a direct path to the gallows.

Through the burning eloquence of his witness, Savonarola attacked his flock's absorption with self-gratification and convenience. His high-placed audience didn't care much for the public criticism; but the common people realized he was preaching the Gospel, and many converted their lives.

Today we bump into the "convenience and pleasure above all" mentality wherever we turn. The philosophy of Feel Good has many adherents. Enough of them occupy places of power, influence, and decision making in our American society.

One of their widely marketed products is abortion on demand, packaged under a label of the right to choose. All Americans and other free peoples understandably love the word "choice" because it seems so essential to liberty. A basic oversight, however, is that we are often limited in what we may choose among. We cannot, for example, choose with impunity to "do drugs" or run a red light, or choose to opt our children out of school programs such as New York City's condom-handout plan. So it isn't really "choose" that is the operative concept here, but the "what" that we choose; the selected item from among alternatives. Too often we get caught up on half of a thought, viz., the action of choosing. We need also to focus on what is the object of that choosing. If our choice results in harm, injury, or death to ourselves or another human being, we have chosen unwisely.

Savonarola tried to make that point to his contemporaries, but they didn't want to hear it. The reformer went so far — perhaps too far — as to encourage good people to pile up their own objects of vanity in a big heap in the city square. Items such as mirrors and combs and perfumes and pornography formed this ad hoc community dump. Then the preacher and the converted would put the torch to the trinkets in what became known as a bonfire of the vanities. Of course, when the zeal of the moment wore off, many went back to the mall for a new set of vanities. And, yes, it's from this event that author Tom Wolfe took the title of his best-selling novel on urban greed and self-absorption.

Savonarola paid the price of living and preaching the Gospel against the scandal of his society and renegade church leaders. Convicted for the usual heresy and treason, he was hanged from a scaffold along with two faithful Dominican companions, their bodies burned at the stake not far from the ashes of the vanities.

While it would be absurd for us to pile up our VCRs, BMWs, and Brie and destroy them, we might be well advised to gather in the plaza of community consciousness and purge some of our own vanities of body and spirit through reflection, prayer, and action. We could start by voicing and voting opposition to the deaths of unborn children directly attributable to someone else's choice.

HOW WE CONTINUE TO KID OURSELVES about the reality of abortion is reflected in the recent episode of New York physician Abu Hayat, who is charged with severing the arm of a baby girl while attempting to abort her. The otherwise healthy child was born hours later. The doctor's error seems to be that he lacked the competence to kill the child. As a result, he's in trouble with the law for having hurt her.

Clearly, the child's death was an acceptable choice to the mother who exercised her court-given "right to choose" when contracting for the abortion. Although her own child's death was sought by the mother, she's now in a snit because the child, Ana Rosa, is damaged. Dead, okay; handicapped, no way.

It's worth noting that within hours after removal of the arm of a fetal non-person, there appeared from the same womb a baby girl person with one arm. Right reason concludes that both the fetus and the baby girl are one-and-the-same individual human person. Logic, as well as biological science, demands that the legally abortable fetus is in fact a living human being, a child, though not yet visible outside the womb. This is the same individual we called fetus (the word means "fruitful; offspring") when she was yawning and hiccuping in the uterus.

Someday Ana Rosa may ask why she has only one arm. How does mom answer that question? Should she tell her daughter of a doctor's inability to perform an abortion that would have eliminated both the question and the questioner? Perhaps someday, while enjoying life, the daughter may pause to thank the doctor without whose clumsy efforts Ana would not be here today. What will be the child's reaction to her own mother who sought this abortion, and to us in society who permit and often encourage such a dark choice? Perhaps the girl will buy the argument that there was nothing personal in the selection of her death; her mother was simply exercising a female's right to choose. When the daughter reaches puberty, she too can choose to abort her own daughter.

Our society demonstrates a growing disregard for human life while waxing compassionate in the slick newspeak of our age. Our easy digestion of soft euphemisms ranging from "choice" to "termination of pregnancy," "product of conception," "non-person," "a bunch of cells," "unwanted tissue," and on and on, expands readily into "quality of life," "death with dignity," "life devoid of value," "artificial nutrition," and even "facilitate expeditious transmogrification." Who knows what tomorrow's menu will include.

In the future, Ana Rosa may face a decision on what to do with a sick or elderly mother. Conveniently, the society that gave us the choice to destroy our own offspring now offers the survivor parity through legal pruning shears by which we can lop riper fruit from the tree of life. Then it's the child's turn to choose.

THIS YEAR WE'VE CELEBRATED the quincentenary of Columbus's first visit to this part of the world. Historians have admonished early European explorers for their harsh treatment of Native American populations. But most agree that among the positive effects of the colonial era was the elimination of human sacrifice in the Americas.

Now, five hundred years later, we find ourselves at odds over its reintroduction.

DURING THE 1970s, American politics gave rise to a noble-sounding but placative phrase so useful to players of verbal dodge ball. The popular qualifier "personally opposed, but . . ." has taken its place alongside another coy Americanism: "Some of my best friends are. . . ."

Today, no other barker of the "personally opposed" moral oxymoron quite matches the eloquence of the sitting governor of the State of New York. Governor Mario Cuomo frowns his personal opposition to abortion, "but. . ." as a skilled political survivor he then retreats from application of his conscience to this public issue lest it be construed as imposition of a moral view. Over the years, the governor appears to have undergone little personal conflict helping to impose taxation and other unpopular presentiments on the populace of his state. Yet on this one issue of innocent human life, he trips over the shadow of self-incrimination.

Has the governor fallen victim to political gymnastics or pandered to special interest groups, or perhaps suffered defects in that renowned logic? How can he in conscientious balance justify a dichotomous position on abortion while at the same time maintaining his unwavering stance on capital punishment?

Before switching on the juice, let me own up to sharing Governor Cuomo's opposition to capital punishment. I too am personally opposed to any state-sanctioned death dealing; no "buts."

Nevertheless, the Supreme Court, which gave us abortion on demand, declared that capital punishment is constitutionally acceptable; it is in effect a right of the state, meaning the people, to apply. Polls continue to show that the people of New York favor an option for capital punishment. Voting within the state legislature consistently demonstrates that the majority of legislators strongly support capital punishment. However, and huzzah! the governor of New York personally opposes the death penalty and steadfastly continues to threaten with veto any relevant legislation. Way to go, Mario!

Yet the governor's firm moral position raises a few questions. Why is he adamant in imposing his personal death-sentence view on the people and legislature of New York when he so readily caves in on abortion? Is the governor not aware that the life in the womb whose death he "personally" opposes but will do nothing to protect is "innocent" of any crime or wrongdoing? Meanwhile, the life of the condemned criminal protected by the governor is recognized as being "guilty" of a heinous crime.

Why the hesitation on the part of the governor? In statements, he asserts his fear that perhaps a criminal sentenced to die *may be* innocent and his death would be a terrible thing. I agree. It happened on Calvary. But why not take that same life-saving position with abortion? All children destroyed in abortion *are* innocent; not "may be" but *are*. The governor doesn't deny their innocence; that's why he personally opposes abortion. Then why allow the innocent to perish?

With capital punishment, the governor finds no essential reason to kill the criminal; nor do I. If there is another way to assure the criminal is removed permanently from society, why kill him/her? A life term in prison without access to parole satisfies the governor. He says we can find other means besides death to deal with the unwanted capital criminal.

But then his logic falters, perhaps for political expediency, as he fails to see that he can take the same approach with the innocent child who will be killed in abortion. What some might term "unwanted children" could be wanted and saved through other means. Certainly, more sensitive efforts are needed to facilitate adoption or the counter-option to keep one's child, through provision of life-giving support to the woman in crisis who, without this support, may see no other alternative than to destroy her own child.

Another governor, who years ago encountered an innocent unwanted by society, had to deal with a tough political choice. Although "personally opposed" to the death of the man, he failed to exert the power of his office to rescue the life being led to execution. Pilate fell into disfavor with ancient Rome and faded away, except in history's long memory of his failure to protect a life he knew to be innocent.

But America offers great opportunities for most of us. Among these are second chances, the opportunity to rethink and change our minds and behavior. Former New York governor Hugh Carey now admits he was wrong to support abortion-related legislation.

Perhaps in time the current New York governor, an intelligent and thoughtful man, may likewise revisit government protection for threatened, innocent human life. As America slaloms down the icy slope to euthanasia, such a heart change could serve him and all of us well in our old age and future infirmities.

SOME FORMS OF CHILD ABUSE PERSIST even after death has claimed the victim. This occurs on either side of the Atlantic. In England, where abortion on demand has flourished since 1965, employees of some clinics routinely feed the bodies of aborted babies into a grinding machine called a "Macerator," which processes tiny corpses into human puree before pouring the remains into the local sewer system.

Now, thanks largely to the efforts of a pro-life Member of Parliament (and a Liberal Democrat, of all things!) named David Alton and a few other concerned MPs, the National Health Minister has assured that the practice will be phased out and replaced by the "more appropriate" method of incineration. This questionable alternative came in response to Alton's demand for an official inquiry into the bizarre pulping practice which he claimed conflicted with government recommendations that aborted fetuses be treated with dignity.

"Until recently," said Alton, "the babies' bodies were thrown into a macerator at a Liverpool abortion clinic — euphemistically called, in a perversion of the English language, the Merseyside Nursing Home.

"After the bodies of the unborn have been crushed and pulped, their remains have been pumped into the public sewers and drains, like human excrement. Some clinics have used this method since 1970."

Now that future Liverpudlians-without-a-future will be incinerated rather than mashed, Alton says a new challenge appears to be in administering the activity. "Health authorities and others are now going to do the dirty work of the clinics; and they will receive blood money, fifty pence (about 90 American cents) per sack."

A trash disposal company with the curious name of "Quick Ways Waste" has contracted with local abortion clinics for transporting the aborted babies to the National Health Service furnace at Liverpool's Walton Hospital. There, the babies will be incinerated with rubbish and general garbage.

This may raise an interesting dilemma for Quick Ways trash haulers, and hospital workers such as porters and incinerator operators who now must participate in the body-disposal process.

According to one London newspaper, the conscience clause of the United Kingdom's 1967 Abortion Act, which permits medical personnel to excuse themselves from abortion-related activity on moral grounds, does not cover other than specifically medical staff. Alton and his pro-life colleagues are exploring a revision to the abortion law's conscience clause to include any person with moral or ethical objections to participation in any aspect of an abortion death.

Mr. Alton exudes British resolve: "Many Members of Parliament believe this is a degrading scandal. Many share my view that, as in sixteen American states, we need laws insisting that the remains of the unborn are treated with respect."

For this purpose, Alton and four other MPs introduced legislation in late 1991 to provide legal protections for the remains of the aborted unborn so that these young innocent dead, in Alton's words, "are accorded dignity; and neither discharged into sewers or thrown into a furnace with the trash."

MP David Alton displays moral stamina. American

law makers could benefit from his example. The truly committed pro-life members of government struggle up the ethical mountain as frustrated as any Sisyphus. In Britain, they've been rolled over many times by the heavy boulder of abortion for more than a quarter-century. Still, they climb and make small gains for life.

Consider the millions of aborted lives lost in this island kingdom. How many Shakespeares have been snuffed out? How many Newtons, Dickenses, Brontës, Churchills? How many Thomas Mores? He, in awaiting death, admonished our concern for convenience and safety: "Do not glory in such futile things but rather in a real joy: that your names are written in the Book of Life. For this really belongs to you, because once you have attained this joy, you cannot lose it, even if all the ranks of demons should struggle against you."

So too is the name of each innocent aborted child, cheated of life as we view it — yet not really; for each human life is fashioned and named by its Creator. Those names are listed forever in the Book of Life and cannot be lost because they are written by the hand of God.

As **AMERICA COUNTS DOWN** to the midnight of our twentieth century, the U.S. Supreme Court continues to bump responsibility for certain abortion-rights decisions back into the laps of state legislatures. In a representative government such as our American republic, that means to some extent putting them back within the grasp of the people. Now, more than ever, the voices of pro-life people need to be heard if we truly wish to return a right to life for all human beings: from conception through natural death.

The focus of abortion activists pro and con shifts once again to our state governments. While many pro-life people will continue to push for a Human Life Amendment to the U.S. Constitution, increased efforts must also go forward to focus more sharply on state and local decision makers.

There now may be a greater expectation for the success of pro-life legislation because home-state lawmakers are within closer earshot. But this only has meaning if pro-lifers commit renewed energies and actions to bring the life message to their representatives, assembly leaders, neighbors, and the press.

In the nearly two decades since Roe v. Wade mandated abortion on demand in the United States, an estimated twenty-seven million innocent young lives have been legally exterminated. Comparisons never effectively describe the reality. Yet more have died from abortion in America in these past two decades than in all the wars of our two-century history.

Few would challenge the assertion that more innocents

have been legally executed since 1973 than have criminals since our nation officially began in 1789.

More innocent human lives were surgically carved up in our clinics and hospitals in the name of "choice" than in any pogroms Dr. Mengele, his colleagues, and his führer ever undertook in the name of obscene expediency.

Just how many geniuses like Beethoven, Shakespeare, Curie, Einstein, Gandhi, and da Vinci have been scraped down the sewer during these "choice" years, only God knows. And only the God of Leviticus and Romans can exact retribution. Our job is to end the bloodshed by effecting societal change through the example of nonviolent love in action.

Unfocused anger will provide neither a solution nor an end to the slaughter of the innocents, nor expunge the crimes of our generation. It is not through violence, but through peaceful direct action, that changes of heart will occur in this land. When America once again regains its wits and ends the pruning of its own next generations, it will be the result of our faithfulness to nonviolent action. Renewal of life values will come from prayer and from what John Cardinal Newman termed "the catching force, the sympathetic influence of what we do." What we do may vary from person to person, but we must do something.

For some, that action will be political: working with legislators, candidates, PACs and other groups to effect change at state and federal levels, and perhaps (one may dream) through a constitutional amendment.

Others will strive to change hearts through public education and advertising as provided through national, state, and local pro-life groups. Some will work in courageously exposed ways by debating and giving talks to school and community groups, teenagers, and adults. These are brave people standing alone in their moral underwear.

Letter writers and pamphleteers reach some eyes and ears, often quite successfully. And, of course, many tenacious, committed pro-life women and men will picket and counsel in rain or shine, sun or snow, year after year to save one mother and her child. Some courageous people will even risk arrest and jail on behalf of those who are being led to their executions.

From what I see of the most visible pro-life people, a combination of these actions form part of their committed agendas. Yet it becomes more evident each day that these actions are often performed as if on a treadmill. We work hard to keep from falling too far behind.

But it's evident that many faithful to life are taking action of another kind. Peaceful, nonviolent actions call numbers of the formerly chary to a personally sacrificial action they may once have derided, or at least feared. It's not an easy course to place one's liberty at peril regardless of the moral rightness of a cause. Yet, like it or not, the rescue has arrived as a pro-life bellwether.

This may not be everyone's cup of tea. But for the pro-life cause to succeed, we must extend at least sufficient intramural tolerance to each other's nonviolent approaches toward the same goal. Otherwise, we make the opposition's task a lot simpler by dividing and internally conquering ourselves. Yet our actions must always remain nonviolent. The God of love, Thomas Merton reminds us, is never glorified by human violence. Contrary to what biased media may publish, Operation Rescue is nonviolent. I've witnessed many rescues, OR and other, over the past decade, and I have never seen any act of violence performed by a rescuer. Yet next day I read in the press that rescuers are violent. The violence I've seen at rescues has come from the protectors of the clinics. It happens that rescuers have been victims of violent response. Bones have been broken and indignities heaped on those who seek to save human lives. Still, the greater violence occurs within the clinics' procedure rooms. There, lives are destroyed and maternal consciences wounded.

Ours is a representative form of government, and our federal and state representatives can only come to know what we their constituents hold dear when we tell them. So tell them. Representatives vote. Majority votes on issues determine the direction the state or nation will take. This tenet is true whether they're debating taxes, education, the environment, or even abortion, infanticide, and euthanasia.

Today's successors to the Supreme Court which created the abortion mess now uneasily nudge the future of legalized abortion in America toward the in-boxes of the individual states. No one likes to be handed a live grenade, so the state legislatures may very well opt to allow the Court's 1973 decision to stand. This would not well serve the cause of life.

We need to tell our freeholders, legislatures, assemblies, Congress, the Senate, and any other elected body of representatives that we expect our elected officials likewise to seek the necessary safeguards for all human life. Else we are prepared to turn them out of office.

But again, representatives won't know this unless enough of us tell them. Each citizen who cares for the protection of innocent human life in America is responsible before God for speaking up in defense of those endangered members of our human family who go unheard or have not yet the voice to speak for themselves.

In THE EARLY 1980s, a young woman named Virginia Robertson was arrested at a peaceful sit-in outside an abortion clinic in Catonsville, Maryland. At her trial, an impatient and cynical judge mocked her: "You wear your religion on your [sleeve]," he said.

"No," replied Ms. Robertson, "I carry it in my heart."

Thank you, Virginia, for the paradigm found. The courage of love-borne witness by this young woman and others like her — to paraphrase the poet — has shot its arrows of peace into our hearts. It is through the vessel of the heart that we first carry our love. We reverence the heart Sacred, and the heart Immaculate. An it is in the silence of our own faithful hearts that God speaks to us.

The word "quiver" bears two meanings. As a verb it connotes trembling, as in fear; but as a noun, quiver is the vessel for arrows, a symbol of strength, armament and — remembering Cupid — even love.

Let our noun quivers take on the mettle of Virginia Robertson and others who put their own liberty at peril for the promptings of their hearts, minds, and souls, and for the sake of the preborn.

Our assignment is to witness to the truth; to tell the Emperor he is naked and to launch peaceful arrows to point this society once again in the direction of life.